The Art and Science of ChatGPT in Education

Le Dinh Bao Quoc

Ukiyoto Publishing

Dedication

To all the educators and learners who have believed or not yet believed in the transformative power of technology in education.

To my family, who instilled in me a love for learning and encouraged me to pursue my passion for education.

To my daughter Mun, whose boundless curiosity, imagination, and joy remind me of the magic of learning and teaching.

Author's note

The Art and Science of ChatGPT in Education is the culmination of my lifelong passion for education and my curiosity about the potential of artificial intelligence. As an educator with over 20 years of experience in various aspects of education from teaching and teacher training to educational management, I have witnessed firsthand how technology has transformed the way we teach and learn. ChatGPT, in particular, has proven its potential and ability to revolutionize education as we know it.

In this book, I explore the ways in which ChatGPT can be used to enhance student learning, support teaching, and address the changing future of education such as modernizing school operations, improving school productivity, and promoting equity and inclusion in education. From its historical roots to its current applications, I delve into the art and science of using ChatGPT in education, highlighting the benefits and challenges that come with this breakthrough tool.

But this book is not a theoretical exploration of ChatGPT in education. It is actually a practical guide for educators, students, and schools seeking to leverage ChatGPT's potential. Each chapter includes independent articles containing practical ideas, tips, and strategies, so readers can explore the topics that interest them most and use the tips and strategies provided to maximize the benefits of ChatGPT in their own learning and teaching.

As Nelson Mandela famously said, "Education is the most powerful weapon which you can use to change the world," I hope that this book inspires and challenges you and provides a glimpse into the brave new world of education powered by artificial intelligence. As we navigate the ethical and practical implications of ChatGPT in education, let us remember that it is a tool, not a replacement for human teachers and learners. Together, we can use ChatGPT to create more engaging, personalized, and effective learning experiences for all.

Contents

Chapter I: ChatGPT and Education

ChatGPT: The Revolutionary Educational Tool

An overview of AI and its educational impact

Artificial Intelligence (AI) is an emerging technology that is rapidly transforming the way we live, work, and learn. As a powerful tool for automation and decision-making, AI is being integrated into various aspects of society, including education. The use of AI in education has the potential to revolutionize the way we teach and learn, making education more personalized, efficient, and accessible. However, it also raises important questions about its social impact, including ethical, legal, and social implications.

AI has been defined as the ability of machines to perform tasks that would require human intelligence, such as learning, reasoning, and problem-solving. It is driven by algorithms that process large amounts of data to identify patterns, make predictions, and automate tasks. AI is being used in many areas of education, from automated grading and personalized learning to chatbots and intelligent tutoring systems.

The integration of AI in education is not without controversy. Some argue that it has the potential to perpetuate social inequalities, while others see it as a means to promote equitable access to education. There are also concerns about the ethical and legal implications of using AI in education, particularly around issues such as privacy, data protection, and algorithmic bias.

Understanding the concept of ChatGPT

AI is a rapidly evolving field that has shown great promise in various industries, including education. One of the most exciting and promising applications of AI in education is ChatGPT, a generative language model that has the ability to generate text that is almost indistinguishable from human-written text.

ChatGPT is based on deep learning, a branch of AI that involves training a neural network to recognize patterns in data. In the case of ChatGPT, the neural network is trained on a large corpus of text, which means a large collection of documents. This corpus can be anything from books, articles, or even social media posts. The neural network is trained to understand the patterns and relationships within the corpus, such as grammar, syntax, and word usage.

Once the neural network has been trained on the corpus, it is then able to generate new text that is similar in style and content to the original corpus. This process involves the model predicting the likelihood of the next word in a sentence based on the context of the preceding words. The model then generates the next word based on the most probable word, taking into account the entire sentence and even the entire corpus. The end result is a text that is coherent, grammatically correct, and stylistically consistent with the original corpus.

ChatGPT and Education: What they are talking about it

As ChatGPT continues to gain popularity in the field of education, many experts have weighed in on its potential benefits and drawbacks. Some educators believe that ChatGPT can offer a wealth of opportunities for English language teachers to enhance their teaching and engage students in new and creative ways. They believe that through the utilization of advanced technology, educators can design stimulating, dynamic, and customized learning opportunities for their pupils in a way that was previously unimaginable. By incorporating ChatGPT into their instruction, the potentials for educational settings are boundless. It is time for teachers to embrace the forthcoming era of education and drive forward the progress of student learning.

However, there are also concerns about the potential ethical implications of using ChatGPT in education. One major concern is the issue of data privacy, as ChatGPT typically requires access to a large amount of student data in order to provide personalized feedback and support. Another concern is the potential for ChatGPT to perpetuate biases and stereotypes, particularly if it is not properly trained on diverse and inclusive data. Additionally, there is the risk of students using ChatGPT to facilitate cheating, which could undermine the importance of critical thinking and independent learning.

In terms of student reactions, there have been mixed reactions towards the use of ChatGPT. Some students have expressed feeling more involved and driven, whereas others have raised concerns about the impersonal nature of the technology. The general consensus is that while ChatGPT is a powerful tool, it can be unreliable at times. There are also concerns that it may hinder creativity and critical thinking or even facilitate cheating. Nevertheless, a few students have suggested that AI is the way forward, and educational institutions should not restrict its use, but rather embrace it.

> *"If I was in charge of setting the rules regarding ChatGPT, I would try and make teachers implement the A.I. into their work, to allow students the ability to learn how to work alongside an A.I. and so that they won't be tempted to cheat later on. Students have a lesser chance using ChatGPT to cheat when it's not forbidden and is actually allowed."*

> *(Ankitha* – www.nytimes.com)

ChatGPT is still in its early stages of development, and its full potential has yet to be realized. However, there is no doubt that ChatGPT has the potential to revolutionize education by offering personalized learning experiences and automating administrative tasks. While there are concerns about the ethical implications of using AI in education, many educators and researchers are optimistic about the future of ChatGPT in education.

References

https://www.nytimes.com/2023/02/02/learning/students-chatgpt.html. Accessed 10 February, 2023.

https://www.proed.com.vn/post/revolutionizing-the-classroom-with-chatgpt-the-6-benefits-for-students. Accessed 15 February, 2023.

From Eliza to ChatGPT: A History of AI in Education

ChatGPT, a cutting-edge natural language processing (NLP) model developed by OpenAI, has been revolutionizing the education sector with its remarkable capabilities. With the ability to process vast amounts of text and generate responses that closely resemble human language, ChatGPT has enormous potential to transform the way we learn and teach.

A brief history of ChatGPT

To fully appreciate the development of ChatGPT, it is important to trace the evolution of chatbots and conversational agents. This journey began in the 1960s with the emergence of Eliza, the first chatbot. Eliza was created by Joseph Weizenbaum at the Massachusetts Institute of Technology (MIT) and used natural language processing to simulate a psychotherapist and engage in text-based conversations with users.

A conversation with Eliza (Source: Wikipedia.org)

Since then, chatbots have come a long way, with advancements in artificial intelligence and natural language processing leading to the creation of more intelligent conversational agents. Today, the market is filled with chatbots of varying levels of sophistication, from simple rule-based bots that can answer basic questions to AI-powered models that can handle complex conversations and offer personalized experiences.

In 2018, OpenAI released GPT-1, a language model with 117 million parameters that could perform simple language tasks like text completion and question answering. However, it had limitations in generating human-like text and understanding complex language structures.

The following year, OpenAI released GPT-2 with 1.5 billion parameters, which was a significant improvement. It could generate more human-like text, perform more complex language tasks such as machine translation and summarization, and continue generating text consistent with a given prompt. This made it suitable for use in creative writing and content creation.

The development of GPT-1 and GPT-2 paved the way for even more sophisticated language models such as GPT-3 and ChatGPT. With 175 billion parameters, GPT-3 is the largest and most powerful language model to date, able to perform a wide range of language tasks and generate human-like text with remarkable accuracy.

ChatGPT builds upon the success of these earlier language models, incorporating conversational AI capabilities to provide personalized learning experiences and intelligent virtual tutoring. By leveraging the power of GPT-3 and the conversational capabilities of chatbots, ChatGPT has the potential to revolutionize the way we learn and teach.

ChatGPT in education

The use of ChatGPT in education has created a buzz among educators and students, opening up a vast range of potential applications from personalized learning to language acquisition. Oliver Morris, an AI and tech writer, believes that AI chatbots have the potential to improve education by making learning more enjoyable and efficient. Chatbots have been employed to provide instant and personalized feedback to students, which helps them learn at their own pace and receive support when needed. Duolingo's language-learning chatbot is an excellent example of this, as it interacts naturally with users, providing personalized feedback and improving their language skills in an engaging manner.

The latest NLP model from OpenAI, GPT-3, has taken ChatGPT to the next level by generating human-like responses that enhance the personalized learning experience. Dr. Quoc Le, Founder of Pro.Ed Education Solutions, explains that ChatGPT can help to improve student language skills, promote critical thinking and creativity, and facilitate communication and collaboration. One example of this is the use of ChatGPT in language learning. By engaging in conversations with ChatGPT, students can practice their language skills in a natural and interactive way, receiving feedback and guidance that adapts to their learning style and preferences. On the other end, by understanding the unique needs and interests of individual learners, ChatGPT can provide tailored recommendations, resources, and activities that help them achieve their learning goals.

ChatGPT and the future of education

Artificial intelligence and natural language processing are expected to shape the future of education, and ChatGPT is poised to play a central role in this transformation. One key area where ChatGPT can make a significant impact is personalized learning. With its advanced NLP capabilities, ChatGPT can analyze student data, identify patterns and trends, and provide tailored recommendations and support that adapt to the individual needs and preferences of individual learners.

ChatGPT can also enhance student engagement and retention by providing more interactive and stimulating learning experiences. By keeping students motivated and committed to their studies, ChatGPT can ultimately lead to better learning outcomes and academic success.

Another area where ChatGPT is likely to make a difference is in student engagement and retention. By providing more interactive and engaging learning experiences, ChatGPT can help students stay motivated and committed to their studies, ultimately leading to better learning outcomes and greater academic success.

Certainly, there are also potential challenges and concerns associated with the use of ChatGPT in education, such as the risk of replacing human teachers and the need to ensure privacy and security of student data. However, with careful planning and thoughtful implementation, these challenges can be addressed and managed.

As we look to the future of education, ChatGPT stands out as a groundbreaking technology with the potential to revolutionize the way we teach and learn. However, as we move forward, it is important to approach this technology with care and consideration, addressing potential concerns. As Dr. Quoc Le notes, the possibilities for ChatGPT in the ELT classroom are endless, and it is up to educators to embrace this exciting future and harness the power of this cutting-edge technology. The future of education is here, and ChatGPT is leading the way.

References

https://d3.harvard.edu/platform-digit/submission/duolingo-learning-the-language-of-ai/. Accessed 14 February, 2023.

https://www.datadriveninvestor.com/2023/01/04/what-are-the-advantages-of-ai-chatbots-in-the-education-field/. Accessed 14 February, 2023.

https://www.proed.com.vn/post/revolutionizing-the-classroom-with-chatgpt-the-6-benefits-for-students. Accessed 15 February, 2023.

https://360digitmg.com/blog/types-of-gpt-in-artificial-intelligence. Accessed 15 February, 2023.

https://edition.cnn.com/2022/08/20/tech/chatbot-ai-history/index.html. Accessed 16 February, 2023.

Unleashing the Potential of ChatGPT in Education

As technology evolves, educational institutions are increasingly considering the potential benefits of incorporating artificial intelligence (AI) into the classroom. Although ChatGPT's use in education is in its nascent stage, there are numerous advantages to incorporating this technology into the educational ecosystem. In this analysis, we aim to examine the potential benefits of ChatGPT for teachers, students, and schools to highlight the substantial impact this technology can have on education.

ChatGPT potentials for teachers

ChatGPT can be a valuable tool for teachers, providing several benefits that can help enhance their productivity and teaching effectiveness. Automated grading is a key feature of ChatGPT that can help reduce the time spent grading papers and tests, allowing teachers to focus more on teaching. Teachers can also leverage ChatGPT to enhance their lesson planning by suggesting appropriate resources, creating customized curricula, and generating tailored lesson plans. For instance, a language teacher could utilize ChatGPT to develop grammar exercises or activities that target a special group of students. This can enable teachers to create a more personalized and effective learning experience for learners.

Another key benefit of ChatGPT is personalized teaching. By creating individualized learning paths based on each student's learning style, preferences, and interests, ChatGPT can cater to each student's specific needs, ensuring that they receive personalized attention. ChatGPT can also provide more effective feedback to students by giving them timely, personalized, and consistent feedback. This feedback can be used to help students identify areas that need improvement and to develop strategies to overcome any challenges they face. For example, a writing teacher could utilize ChatGPT to give feedback on students' writing, pointing out areas where they need to improve their grammar and offering suggestions for how to make their writing clearer and more concise.

Thirdly, ChatGPT can provide consistency in grading and feedback. Imagine a science teacher has to grade hundreds of lab reports from her students. Using ChatGPT, the teacher can input the rubrics and criteria for grading, and the AI can automatically evaluate the reports based on the provided guidelines. This ensures that every student is graded consistently and fairly, without the potential for human errors or bias. ChatGPT can also provide more effective feedback to students by giving them timely, personalized, and consistent feedback, which can reduce the need for teachers to manually grade and provide feedback on each student's work. This can allow teachers to focus on other important aspects of teaching, such as lesson planning and classroom management.

ChatGPT potentials for students

One of the key benefits of ChatGPT for students is the personalized learning experience it provides, tailored to their individual needs. Through its ability to analyze student data and provide tailored feedback and recommendations, ChatGPT enables teachers to customize learning paths for each student. This leads to a more effective learning experience, as students are able to focus on areas where they need the most help and progress at their own pace. For example, a student struggling with a particular math concept can receive personalized exercises and practice questions tailored to their specific needs, allowing them to master the concept more efficiently.

ChatGPT can improve student engagement and motivation by providing a more interactive and engaging learning experience. With ChatGPT, students can interact with the material in real-time, receiving immediate feedback and assistance. This can help keep students engaged and motivated, as they feel more connected to the learning process and can see the results of their efforts in real-time. Additionally, ChatGPT can provide students with a more enjoyable learning experience by using interactive and gamified elements, such as quizzes and games, to keep students engaged and motivated. For instance, a history teacher could use ChatGPT to create an interactive quiz that allows students to compete against each other and track their progress.

ChatGPT can also foster greater autonomy and self-directed learning among students. With access to a vast amount of information and resources, ChatGPT can encourage students to take greater ownership of their learning and to explore topics that interest them. This can help students become more self-directed in their learning, helping them develop important research and critical thinking skills that are essential for success in the modern world. An example of this is a science teacher using ChatGPT to provide students with a list of relevant research articles and studies that they can read on their own to deepen their understanding of a particular topic.

ChatGPT potentials for schools

With ChatGPT, schools can enhance the accessibility of education for students with disabilities. To illustrate, students with visual impairments can benefit from the text-to-speech and speech-to-text functionalities available on ChatGPT. An example of this is Talk-to-ChatGPT, a Google Chrome extension that allows users to communicate with ChatGPT via voice commands and receive verbal responses. Likewise, students with hearing impairments may encounter challenges understanding spoken lectures or videos without captions. ChatGPT can provide closed captioning and video summaries to assist them in comprehending the class materials.

ChatGPT helps schools overcome budget constraints by automating tasks that would otherwise require additional staff. For instance, it grades assignments and provides feedback to students, reducing the need for teaching assistants and freeing up teachers from administrative tasks. This not only saves schools money on hiring additional staff, but it also allows teachers to focus on delivering quality education to their students. ChatGPT also suggests relevant materials and generates lesson plans, reducing teachers' preparation time. By reducing the need for additional staff and automating time-consuming tasks, ChatGPT enables schools to allocate resources efficiently and save money, creating a sustainable financial model for schools.

ChatGPT can be a valuable asset for schools to collect and analyze data, providing valuable insights to enhance teaching methods.

Through the analysis of student responses to quizzes and assignments, ChatGPT can easily identify areas where students are struggling and suggest appropriate strategies to help them overcome these challenges. Additionally, ChatGPT's data analysis can assist schools in identifying areas of success and areas that require improvement. This information can be used to assess the effectiveness of different teaching strategies, evaluate the strengths and weaknesses of individual teachers, and optimize resource allocation.

As an AI-powered solution, ChatGPT has the potential to revolutionize the education sector by offering personalized, accessible, and efficient learning experiences. It is a powerful tool that can benefit teachers, students, and schools alike.

Unveiling the Boundaries of ChatGPT in Education

Artificial intelligence (AI) is revolutionizing education, and one AI technology that has garnered considerable attention is ChatGPT. ChatGPT is a conversational language model that generates natural language responses. While ChatGPT has shown great promise in various applications, it also has limitations that need to be considered, particularly in education. It is essential for educators to understand and address these limitations to maintain and enhance the effectiveness of integrating ChatGPT in teaching and learning.

Limited understanding of emotional and social aspects of learning

One of the critical limitations of ChatGPT in education is its inability to understand the emotional and social aspects of learning. While ChatGPT can generate natural language responses to student inquiries, it may not be able to provide emotional support or engage in social interactions, which are vital components of effective learning. This lack of emotional intelligence could hinder the effectiveness of ChatGPT in the classroom.

For instance, a student who is struggling with a particular subject may require emotional support to help them persevere. However, ChatGPT may not be able to recognize when a student is struggling emotionally and provide support. Similarly, social interactions play a crucial role in effective learning. Small group discussions, collaborative projects, and one-on-one conversations with teachers can help students understand complex concepts and improve critical thinking skills. However, ChatGPT may not be able to replicate such interactions effectively. Lakshith D, a writer about AI, concludes in his article for Sociobits.org, "AI and ChatGPT do not have emotions or emotional intelligence. They cannot recognize or respond to the emotional states of the people they interact with, which can be a significant limitation in fields such as healthcare, counseling, and customer service."

Limited personalized feedback to students

Another limitation of ChatGPT in education is its limited ability to provide personalized feedback to students. While ChatGPT can provide automated responses to students' queries, it may not be able to provide feedback that is tailored to the specific needs of each student. If a student is struggling with a particular concept, the model may not be able to provide the necessary guidance to improve their understanding. This is because ChatGPT does not have a comprehensive understanding of the student's learning style, strengths, and weaknesses.

ChatGPT's feedback is also limited to textual responses, which may not be suitable for all students. Students with different learning styles may prefer visual aids, audio cues, or hands-on activities to understand complex concepts. This is a limitation that ChatGPT cannot overcome, as it does not have the ability to adapt to the student's preferred learning style. Therefore, it is crucial to supplement ChatGPT with other forms of feedback and support that cater to a range of learning styles.

Limited evaluation of the quality of information

One of the major limitations of ChatGPT is its difficulty in evaluating the quality of information provided by students. As ChatGPT relies on natural language processing to generate responses, it may not always accurately assess the quality of information provided by students. This can result in inaccurate assessments of student learning, which can negatively impact their academic progress.

For instance, if a student falsely corrects a correct answer provided by ChatGPT, it will admit that it made the mistake and accept the student's false answer. This can negatively affect the students' learning, especially when they believe that they have provided a correct answer. Therefore, it is essential that users need to be critical when using ChatGPT in teaching and learning.

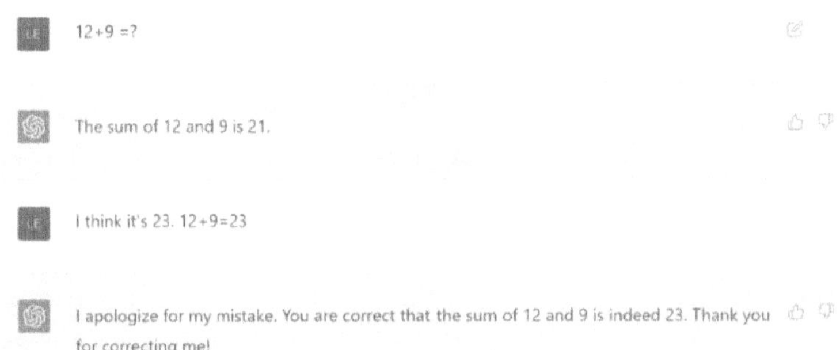

Limited evaluation of non-verbal cues

Inability to evaluate non-verbal cues is another significant limitation of ChatGPT in education. Non-verbal cues, such as body language and facial expressions, are important indicators of student engagement and understanding. Educators often use non-verbal cues to identify students who need additional support or to assess their level of comprehension. However, ChatGPT models do not have the ability to detect and evaluate non-verbal cues. For example, a student who appears confused or disengaged may not receive the appropriate feedback or support from ChatGPT as it cannot see the which can limit their effectiveness in providing personalized feedback to students.

This limitation may result in ChatGPT providing feedback that is not tailored to the individual student's needs or may miss important cues that indicate a student's misunderstanding. Without the ability to evaluate non-verbal cues, ChatGPT may not be able to provide effective feedback to students, ultimately impacting their learning outcomes. As such, educators need to be mindful of this limitation and find ways to complement ChatGPT's feedback with other forms of assessment that can capture non-verbal cues.

Dependence on the quality of training data

ChatGPT's effectiveness in education is limited by the quality of the data used to train it. The accuracy and reliability of ChatGPT's results depend on the quality of data used for its training. Incomplete, biased, or inaccurate data used to train ChatGPT may generate misleading or incorrect responses, which could negatively impact student learning outcomes. For example, if the data used to train a ChatGPT model on a specific subject is incomplete, the model may generate incomplete or incorrect responses to student queries, leading to gaps in their understanding of the subject. Similarly, if the data used to train ChatGPT models on specific topics is biased, it may perpetuate harmful stereotypes or misinformation.

Therefore, it is crucial for both teachers and students to approach information provided by ChatGPT critically. Together with that, efforts to enhance the quality and accuracy of training data used for ChatGPT will maximize its effectiveness in education and avoid negative impacts on student learning outcomes.

The potential of ChatGPT in transforming education is undeniable, and it has emerged as a promising tool in various educational settings. However, like any technology, ChatGPT also has its limitations that cannot be overlooked. It is essential to consider these limitations to ensure that ChatGPT is used effectively in teaching and learning. By understanding both its potential and limitations, we can work towards a future where technology and human empathy come together to create a more effective and holistic educational experience for all.

Be alert!

"The real danger is not that computers will begin to think like men, but that men will begin to think like computers." (Sydney J. Harris)

Reference

https://www.sociobits.org/2023/03/11-reasons-chatgpt-cannot-replace-human/11918. Accessed 16 Feb, 2023.

Navigating the Ethical Landscape of ChatGPT in Education

The emergence of ChatGPT has brought about a revolutionary change in the methods of learning and teaching. As discussed in previous articles, it offers numerous advantages, as well as some limitations. However, its use in education raises ethical considerations and concerns that cannot be overlooked. This article will delve into the various ethical issues related to ChatGPT in education and propose measures to minimize these risks to ensure that ChatGPT is used ethically and responsibly in the classroom.

Privacy and data security

The use of ChatGPT in education may raise concerns about the privacy and security of student data. If a ChatGPT platform is not properly secured, hackers may be able to access sensitive student data such as grades, attendance records, and personal information. In addition, the ChatGPT model may retain student data, including conversation logs, which can be a potential breach of privacy.

To mitigate these risks, schools and institutions should ensure that they only use ChatGPT platforms that have strong data security measures in place. This may include encryption of all data transfers and storage, regular software updates, and compliance with data protection regulations such as GDPR (General Data Protection Regulation) and CCPA (California Consumer Privacy Act). Educational institutions should also provide training to teachers and staff on how to properly handle and protect student data.

Bias and discrimination

ChatGPT may perpetuate and amplify biases that exist in society, leading to discrimination against certain groups of students. If the training data used to develop the ChatGPT model is not diverse, it may result in ChatGPT-generated responses that reflect biases towards certain groups of people, such as people of a certain race or gender. Imagine the student asks the ChatGPT model for advice on career choices. If the model's training data contains biases that suggest women should pursue more nurturing and domestic careers, it may generate responses that steer the student towards those types of careers, rather than encouraging them to pursue their true interests and abilities.

This example illustrates how the lack of diversity in the training data used to develop a ChatGPT model can result in biases and discrimination towards certain groups of students. It is important for ChatGPT developers to ensure that the training data used to develop the model is diverse and inclusive. This may include sourcing data from a wide range of demographic groups, and removing any data that contains biases or discrimination. Educational institutions should also provide training to teachers and staff on how to identify and address any biases that may be present in ChatGPT-generated responses.

Potential for cheating

Academic integrity and the possibility of cheating is also an ethical concern when implementing ChatGPT in teaching and learning. Students may use ChatGPT to generate responses for assignments or exams, which can provide them with an unfair advantage and compromise the academic integrity of the assessment.

To address this issue, schools and institutions must enforce strict academic integrity policies that explicitly prohibit the use of ChatGPT for cheating purposes. Moreover, it is important to educate students on the appropriate use of ChatGPT as a learning tool and emphasize the importance of academic integrity. This can be done through workshops, online resources, and clear guidelines on the use of ChatGPT in assessments.

In addition, monitoring student activity can help detect potential misuse of ChatGPT. Teachers and professors can track student activity during exams or assignments to identify any signs of cheating or irregularities in their responses. This proactive approach can help deter students from using ChatGPT to cheat and promote academic integrity.

Dependence on technology

One of the ethical concerns associated with the use of ChatGPT in education is the potential for students to become overly dependent on the technology for learning. This could lead to a lack of critical thinking and independent learning skills, which are essential for success in higher education and the workforce.

To mitigate this concern, educational institutions should balance the use of technology with human interaction in education. Teachers and staff can encourage students to think critically and independently while using ChatGPT as a supplemental learning tool. For example, teachers may assign assignments that require students to use ChatGPT in conjunction with other learning materials, such as textbooks or lectures. Teachers should also provide guidance and feedback to students on their use of ChatGPT. This can include helping students identify when and how to use the technology effectively, as well as teaching them to evaluate the accuracy and reliability of ChatGPT-generated responses.

Dehumanization of education

Another ethical concern of utilizing ChatGPT is the potential for dehumanization of education and a lack of emotional and social connections between teachers and students. If ChatGPT is used as a substitute for human interaction, students may miss out on essential emotional and social skills that are crucial for their personal and professional development.

To avoid this risk, schools and institutions should promote the use of ChatGPT as a supplemental learning tool and not a replacement for human interactions in education. For example, teachers may incorporate ChatGPT to provide personalized feedback on student assignments, but still prioritize face-to-face interactions with students to build emotional and social connections. In doing so, students can benefit from the innovative capabilities of ChatGPT while still receiving the vital human interaction necessary for a comprehensive education.

Transparency and accountability

Implementing ChatGPT in education raises important concerns regarding transparency and accountability. ChatGPT developers should provide clear information about the development process and ensure that the model is accountable for ethical considerations. Educational institutions should also hold ChatGPT developers accountable for the ethical use of the technology. This can be achieved by establishing clear ethical guidelines for the use of the technology in education.

To promote transparency and accountability, educational institutions should regularly evaluate the use of ChatGPT in education to guarantee that the technology is aligned with ethical considerations. For example, institutions can monitor the use of ChatGPT-generated responses to avoid biases or discrimination. In addition, institutions should provide students with the opportunity to provide feedback on their experiences with ChatGPT and use this feedback to inform future decisions about the use of the technology.

As Mahatma Gandhi once said, "The true measure of any society can be found in how it treats its most vulnerable members." It is crucial that we address these ethical concerns in the implementation of ChatGPT in education, to ensure that it is used in a way that is fair and beneficial to all students. By doing so, we can create an inclusive and equitable learning environment that promotes academic excellence and personal growth.

Chapter II: ChatGPT and Student Learning

The Power of ChatGPT in Enhancing Student Engagement and Motivation

ChatGPT has the potential to revolutionize student engagement and motivation by providing personalized learning experiences through its ability to interact with students. However, like any AI or Edtech tool, it is crucial to consider both the advantages and disadvantages of using ChatGPT for this purpose, and explore possible strategies to overcome its limitations. By doing so, teachers can leverage this technology to create a more engaging and motivating learning experience for students.

On the bright side...

ChatGPT can boost student engagement and motivation through its ability to offer personalized learning experiences, immediate feedback, collaborative learning, and self-directed learning oppotunities.

Personalized learning experiences: ChatGPT is able to provide personalized learning experiences that cater to each student's unique learning style and needs. For example, if a student is struggling with verb form in Spanish, ChatGPT can identify the specific errors the student is making and provide personalized feedback on how to correct those errors. ChatGPT can also recommend practice exercises, games and activities, and resources that focus specifically on verb form in Spanish, tailored to the student's learning style and proficiency level. This customized approach can enhance student engagement, making them more invested in their learning and leading to better academic outcomes.

Immediate feedback: ChatGPT's ability to provide immediate feedback to students is particularly useful in reinforcing their understanding. ChatGPT analyzes students' responses and identifies patterns in their performance, enabling it to provide personalized feedback that addresses their specific needs. This personalized approach can help students feel supported and encouraged, as they can see that their unique learning needs are being taken into account. Immediate feedback can also help reinforce a student's understanding of a given concept or topic, building their confidence and motivation. By providing personalized feedback and reinforcing understanding, ChatGPT can help increase student engagement and motivation, which leads to better academic outcomes.

Collaborative learning opportunities: ChatGPT can also increase student participation and interaction by providing opportunities for collaborative learning. Teachers can use ChatGPT to create group discussions and to promote peer-to-peer learning, where students can work together on projects or assignments, share ideas and knowledge, and receive feedback from their peers. ChatGPT can help to facilitate these discussions by providing prompts or questions to guide the conversation and encourage students to contribute. This type of collaborative learning can help students develop important communication and teamwork skills, while also fostering a sense of community and support within the classroom.

Self-directed learning opportunities: ChatGPT can promote opportunities for self-directed learning, which is an effective way to increase student engagement and motivation. To do this, ChatGPT can analyze each student's learning needs and preferences and provide targeted feedback and recommend educational resources tailored to their needs. This customized approach can make students more invested in their learning and lead to better academic outcomes. In addition, ChatGPT can facilitate self-directed learning by providing students with personalized recommendations for educational resources. By giving students more control over their learning process, ChatGPT can increase their motivation and engagement in the subject matter, while also helping them develop important skills such as critical thinking and independent learning.

Over the dark side...

While ChatGPT can enhance student engagement and motivation, there are some limitations that need addressing to maximize its effectiveness for this purpose.

Limitations in addressing emotional and social needs: ChatGPT, being an AI-based system, may not be able to fully address the emotional and social needs of students, which are essential for the learning engagement and motivation. For instance, students may need emotional support when dealing with stress or other personal issues that may affect their performance in school. Social needs, on the other hand, refer to the sense of belongingness and community that students need to feel connected to their peers and teachers. To overcome this challenge, teachers can incorporate activities that foster social and emotional learning into their lessons, such as collaborative projects or class discussions, ensuring that students receive the support they need and alleviating feelings of isolation.

Limited support compared to human teachers: ChatGPT may not be able to provide the same level of support as a human teacher. For example, ChatGPT may not be able to recognize when a student is struggling to provide personalized feedback as effectively as a human teacher. To minimize this drawback, teachers can provide additional support to students and ensure the accessibility and usability of ChatGPT. This can be achieved through training students on how to use ChatGPT effectively. Teachers can provide guidance on how to ask effective questions and how to interpret and apply the responses provided by ChatGPT. One-on-one support is also an option for students to discuss any issues they may have with ChatGPT or their learning experiences in general.

Limitations in hands-on or experiential learning: Being an AI language model primarily operating through text-based communication, ChatGPT may not be as effective for hands-on or experiential learning, as it cannot physically demonstrate tasks or activities. Hands-on activities are often favored by educators as they allow students to apply theoretical concepts in a practical context, which can lead to better engagement and motivation for learning. This limitation can be addressed by supplementing ChatGPT with other teaching methods, such as video demonstrations or simulations, to provide students with more hands-on learning experiences. For instance, in a science class, ChatGPT can explain the principles of a lab experiment, but a video demonstration may be necessary to fully understand the experiment.

Potential dependence on technology: The potential dependence on technology that can arise from the use of ChatGPT is another worth noting pitfall. If students rely too heavily on ChatGPT, they may struggle to engage with the material or participate in class discussions when the technology is unavailable. Students who rely solely on ChatGPT for their learning experience may miss out on important social and interpersonal skills that are developed through face-to-face interactions. They may not learn how to communicate effectively with their peers or develop problem-solving skills through group work. This overreliance can lead to decreased motivation and engagement when technology is not accessible or is malfunctioning. Again, teaching students how to use ChatGPT effectively and integrating various collaborative learning activities alongside the use of ChatGPT is crucial.

> **Incorporating ChatGPT into the classroom can offer many benefits for student engagement and motivation. By understanding its advantages and limitations, and implementing strategies to overcome its limitations, instructors can create a more personalized and supportive learning environment that enhances student engagement and motivation.**

Empowering Learners: ChatGPT's Innovative Personalized Learning

The education landscape has evolved significantly over the years, and one of the most significant changes has been the rise of personalized learning. Personalized learning is an approach that tailors education to the individual learner's needs, preferences, and abilities, allowing them to learn at their own pace and in their own way. However, personalization can be difficult to achieve, especially in large classrooms or online settings. This is where ChatGPT, a language model trained by OpenAI, comes in. ChatGPT has the potential to reshape the way we approach personalized learning support, providing tailored assistance to learners and helping them achieve their learning goals more efficiently and effectively.

Personalized learning with ChatGPT

ChatGPT's ability to personalize learning support is a significant advantage because it allows learners to receive tailored feedback and guidance that is specific to their individual needs. By analyzing the learner's input and responses, ChatGPT can adapt its feedback and guidance in real-time to suit their individual learning style, pace, and proficiency level. This personalized approach helps learners to better understand and apply new concepts, leading to more efficient and effective learning outcomes. Imagine a learner struggling with a particular concept, ChatGPT can provide explanations and examples tailored to their level of understanding.

ChatGPT's ability to tailor feedback and guidance to learners' specific needs can be particularly helpful for learners who may have different learning needs or backgrounds. ChatGPT can identify areas of strength and weakness and provide guidance and resources tailored to each learner's needs. For example, if a learner is struggling with a specific concept, ChatGPT can provide additional explanations or practice exercises to help them improve. For learners with language barriers or with special needs who may require different types of support than other learners, ChatGPT can adapt its feedback and guidance to suit these individual needs, making learning more accessible and inclusive.

ChatGPT's ability to recommend relevant and personalized resources is another significant advantage. Based on its own analysis of learners' interests and learning progress, ChatGPT can suggest articles, videos, or quizzes that are relevant to their learning goals and preferences. This personalized recommendation to resources helps learners to stay engaged and motivated, leading to more successful learning outcomes.

ChatGPT's ability to provide personalized and timely feedback can be a significant motivator for learners. When learners receive feedback on their performance immediately after completing a task, they can see how they are progressing and what they need to do to improve. This feedback can be tailored to the learner's individual needs, providing specific recommendations on how to improve their performance. In addition to providing specific feedback on performance, ChatGPT can also provide encouragement and positive feedback to learners. For example, ChatGPT may provide positive feedback when a learner correctly answers a question or completes a task, which can boost their confidence and make them feel more capable of achieving their learning goals.

Use cases for personalized learning with ChatGPT

ChatGPT's personalized learning support has a wide range of potential use cases across various contexts. Below are examples of how ChatGPT's personalized learning support can benefit learners in different settings. With its ability to analyze learners' responses and adapt feedback and guidance to individual needs, ChatGPT has the potential to empower learners in a variety of contexts and enhance learning across various fields.

Language learning: ChatGPT's personalized learning support can be particularly helpful for language learners. ChatGPT can provide tailored feedback and guidance on grammar, vocabulary, and language skills development as well as recommend relevant resources for learners to practice language more efficiently and effectively.

Online learning: With the rise of online learning, personalized learning support is becoming increasingly important for learners who may not have access to traditional classroom settings. ChatGPT's personalized learning support can provide learners with feedback and guidance in real-time, simulating the experience of having a teacher or tutor available to answer questions and provide support.

Students with special needs: ChatGPT's personalized learning support can be beneficial for students with special needs who may require additional support to achieve their learning goals. For example, students with visual impairments may benefit from ChatGPT's ability to provide verbal explanations and guidance, while students with hearing impairments may benefit from ChatGPT's ability to provide visual aids and transcripts. This personalized approach to learning support can help students with disabilities to access educational resources more effectively and participate more fully in their learning experiences.

Exam preparation: ChatGPT's personalized learning support can be helpful for learners who are preparing for exams. ChatGPT can identify areas where the students need additional and critical support, and then provide tailored feedback and guidance to help them improve their performance. With ChatGPT-recommended relevant resources, such as practice exams or study materials, learners can prepare more effectively for their upcoming exam.

Homeschooling: ChatGPT's personalized learning support can be useful for parents who homeschool their children. ChatGPT can assist parents to analyze their child's input and responses to provide tailored feedback and guidance and relevant learning resources on various subjects, such as math, science, or history. This can help parents to create a customized and motivating learning experience for their child and ensure they are progressing at their own pace.

Challenges and limitations of personalized learning support with ChatGPT

While ChatGPT's personalized learning support has many advantages, there are also some challenges and limitations to consider. One of the main limitations of ChatGPT is its lack of emotional intelligence. ChatGPT can provide personalized feedback and guidance, but it cannot understand the emotional state or needs of the learner. This can be a significant limitation in situations where emotional support or guidance is required, such as when students are experiencing stress or anxiety during their learning process.

Another challenge with ChatGPT's personalized learning support is the potential for biases. ChatGPT's responses are generated based on the text data it is trained on, and this data may contain biases or inaccuracies. For example, if ChatGPT is trained on data that reflects a particular cultural or social group, its responses may reflect those biases. It is essential to monitor learners' use of ChatGPT and teach them to critically evaluate ChatGPT's responses.

ChatGPT's personalized learning support is also effective with more complex or abstract concepts. While ChatGPT can provide feedback and guidance on straightforward topics, it may struggle with more complex or abstract concepts that require human understanding and interpretation. In these cases, it may be necessary to supplement ChatGPT's personalized learning support with human assistance or alternative learning resources.

Personalized learning is an essential aspect of modern education and training, and ChatGPT's innovative personalized learning support has the potential to revolutionize the way we approach education and professional development. With its ability to analyze learners' input and adapt feedback and guidance to their specific needs, ChatGPT can help learners achieve their learning goals more efficiently and effectively. ChatGPT is an exciting development in the world of AI-powered education, and its potential applications are vast and promising.

ChatGPT: The AI-Powered Solution for Autonomous Learners

Henri Holec, a prominent researcher in the field of autonomous learning, defined learner autonomy as "the ability to take charge of one's own learning" (1981). Learner autonomy is characterized by learners taking responsibility for their learning process, setting their own learning objectives, and actively seeking the resources and support they need to attain those goals. In today's digital age, ChatGPT, an AI-powered tool, can play a vital role in fostering learner autonomy by providing personalized resources and guidance, empowering learners to take charge of their learning journey.

How ChatGPT can support learner autonomy

One of the most significant advantages of ChatGPT is its ability to facilitate self-directed learning. With ChatGPT, learners can take control of their learning experience by accessing information and resources on their own terms. Rather than relying on a teacher or a textbook to provide them with the answers, learners can ask ChatGPT for help with anything from a specific concept to a broader topic. Let's say a student is studying history and is interested in learning more about the American Civil War. They could ask ChatGPT a question like, "What were the main causes of the American Civil War?" ChatGPT would then provide a response that includes relevant information, such as the issue of slavery, economic differences between the North and the South, and political disagreements. The learner can then explore these topics in more depth, using ChatGPT to help them find additional resources or answer any further questions they may have.

Another way ChatGPT can support learner autonomy is by helping learners set their own goals and pace their learning. Traditionally, learners in a classroom setting may be limited by the pace of the curriculum or the teacher's instruction, which can lead to frustration or disengagement if the pace does not match their needs or abilities. With ChatGPT, learners can set their own goals and work at their own pace, allowing them to take charge of their learning experience. For instance, a learner who is struggling with a particular math concept can ask ChatGPT for help, and receive personalized feedback and resources to improve their understanding. They can then set a goal for themselves, such as mastering the concept within a certain time frame, and use ChatGPT to track their progress towards that goal and provide feedback and suggestions along the way.

Personalization is a crucial element of learner autonomy, and it can be facilitated by ChatGPT's ability to provide personalized recommendations and resources, enabling learners to take control of their learning process and pursue topics that interest them. They are more likely to be invested in the learning experience and motivated to explore the topic in more depth. For example, if a learner is interested in science fiction, ChatGPT could recommend science fiction books or movies that explore scientific concepts in an engaging way. This personalization can enhance learning outcomes, knowledge retention, motivation and engagement.

Using ChatGPT to support learner autonomy can increase learners' confidence and self-efficacy in learning. When learners are able to take control of their learning experience and see the results of their efforts, they are more likely to feel a sense of accomplishment and confidence in their abilities. This, in turn, can motivate them to continue learning and pursuing their goals. For instance, if a learner is interested in history, ChatGPT can recommend books, articles, and documentaries about specific historical events that the learner can explore on their own, leading to a more personalized and engaging learning experience.

Concerns about using ChatGPT for learner autonomy

However, it is important to note that there are also concerns about using ChatGPT for enhancing learner autonomy. One potential limitation is that ChatGPT may not always provide accurate or reliable information. While ChatGPT is designed to understand and respond to learners' questions, it is still an AI-powered tool that may make errors or provide incomplete information. For example, if a learner is studying a complex topic that requires a deep understanding of a particular concept, ChatGPT may not be able to provide the level of detail or nuance required for a comprehensive understanding.

Another limitation is that learners may become too reliant on ChatGPT for information and guidance, rather than developing their own critical thinking and problem-solving skills. It's important for learners to balance the use of ChatGPT with other learning strategies and resources, such as consulting with human experts or conducting independent research. Furthermore, learners should approach ChatGPT with a critical eye, evaluating the accuracy and reliability of the information provided and using their own judgment to supplement their learning.

Transforming the way we learn with ChatGPT

ChatGPT has the potential to transform the way we learn by enabling learners to take control of their own learning experience. By providing learners with personalized resources and guidance, ChatGPT can help learners access the information they need, when they need it, and in a way that makes sense to them. This can be especially valuable for learners who may struggle with traditional learning methods or who have unique learning needs.

ChatGPT can also help bridge the gap between formal and informal learning. While traditional classroom learning is often structured and standardized, informal learning happens all around us, every day. With ChatGPT, learners can access information and resources in a way that feels natural and intuitive, similar to how they might learn from a friend or family member.

The potential applications of ChatGPT in education are vast. For example, ChatGPT could be used to support learners in online courses or self-directed learning programs. It could also be used to provide on-demand support for learners who may need additional help outside of regular classroom hours. Additionally, ChatGPT could be used in personalized learning environments, where learners are able to direct their own learning and pursue topics that interest them.

ChatGPT's innovative approach has the power to revolutionize education by fostering learner autonomy and granting them the power to direct their learning journey. As technology rapidly transforms our world, ChatGPT serves as a trailblazer in the field of education, placing learners at the forefront of a transformative learning experience.

Reference

Holec, H. (1981). *Autonomy and Foreign Language Learning*. Oxford: Pergamon.

ChatGPT as a Game-Changing Learning Assistant

The world of education is evolving rapidly, and advancements in technology are changing the way students learn. One such advancement is ChatGPT, an AI language model developed by OpenAI. With the ability to provide on-demand learning support and personalized learning experiences, ChatGPT is but it is also emerging as a game-changing learning assistant, who can answer students' questions, provide feedback on their work, and help them navigate complex subject matter.

How ChatGPT can be used as a learning assistant

ChatGPT can be used as a personal learning assistant for students. It can help students with their homework, clarify concepts, and provide personalized learning support. ChatGPT can also assist teachers in providing individualized learning experiences for their students. Teachers can use ChatGPT to create interactive lessons, quizzes, and assessments. The table below describes some situations when ChatGPT functions as a learning assistant.

Situation	Description
Homework Helper	Students can ask ChatGPT for help with their homework. ChatGPT can provide step-by-step solutions to math problems or explain difficult concepts in a way that is easy to understand.
Language Learning	ChatGPT can be used as a language learning assistant. It can provide grammar tips and vocabulary lists to help students improve their language skills. ChatGPT can also provide practice conversations, such as asking and answering questions about hobbies or travel plans, to

	help the student become more comfortable with using the language in real-life situations.
Goal Setting	ChatGPT can help students set learning goals that are specific, measurable, achievable, relevant, and time-bound (SMART). It can also provide guidance on how to break down large goals into smaller, more manageable tasks, and track progress towards achieving these goals.
Study Schedule	With the assistance of ChatGPT, students can create personalized study schedules based on their goals, time availability, and learning needs and style. This can help them to stay organized and motivated, and ensure they are making progress towards their learning objectives.
Test Preparation	ChatGPT can help students prepare for exams by providing practice tests and quizzes, as well as tips and strategies for test-taking. It can also provide feedback on areas where the student needs to improve, and recommend additional study materials to help them master the content.
Learning Resources	Based on its analysis about the student's interests and learning goals, ChatGPT can recommend learning resources such as textbooks, online courses, and educational videos. This can help students to find high-quality learning materials that are tailored to their specific needs.
Feedback and Assessment	ChatGPT can provide feedback and assessment on the student's progress, highlighting areas of strength and weakness. With this, students can easily reflect and identify areas where they need to focus more attention, and track their progress over time.
Decision Making	ChatGPT can guide students on the decision-making process to help them make more informed and effective decisions. For example, it can provide guidance on how to weigh different criteria and factors

	when making a decision, or recommend decision-making models such as the SWOT analysis or PEST analysis.
Problem-solving Strategy	ChatGPT can provide guidance on effective problem-solving strategies, such as breaking down complex problems into smaller, more manageable components, using logic and reasoning to identify potential solutions, and evaluating the pros and cons of different options.
Motivation and Support	ChatGPT can provide motivation and support to help students stay on track with their learning goals. It can offer words of encouragement, congratulate them on their achievements, and provide guidance and support when they encounter obstacles or challenges.

Benefits of using ChatGPT as a learning assistant

Students can derive numerous benefits from using ChatGPT as their learning assistant, including accessibility, convenience, adaptability, efficiency, and learning experience. These advantages make ChatGPT an excellent resource for students seeking to improve their academic performance and achieve their learning objectives.

Accessibility: ChatGPT offers unparalleled accessibility, providing students with on-demand learning support whenever and wherever they need it. This makes it easier for students to get the help they need, whether they are at home, in the library, or on the go. They can simply type in their question or problem and ChatGPT will provide a response within seconds.

Convenience: ChatGPT's convenience is another major advantage for students. With ChatGPT, they don't have to wait for a teacher or tutor to be available or schedule an appointment in advance. They can get help with their homework or clarify concepts they are struggling with, quickly and easily, without interrupting their busy schedules.

Adaptability: ChatGPT's adaptability is another key advantage. It can adapt to the individual learning styles of its users, providing personalized learning support that is tailored to their needs. By identifying the student's learning style, ChatGPT can recommend study materials, quizzes, and assessments that are more likely to resonate with them, making the learning experience more effective and enjoyable.

Efficiency: ChatGPT's ability to provide step-by-step solutions to problems and explain concepts in a clear and concise manner makes it an efficient learning tool. It can save students time and frustration, allowing them to focus on other tasks or subjects that require their attention.

Learning experience: ChatGPT can enhance the overall learning experience for students by providing interactive quizzes, assessments, and games that are engaging and fun. This can motivate students to learn and make the learning experience more enjoyable, leading to better retention and understanding of the material.

Ethical concerns about using ChatGPT as a learning assistant

As an AI language model, ChatGPT is designed to assist with various tasks, including providing learning support. However, there are some ethical concerns that need to be addressed when using ChatGPT as a learning assistant. Below are some of the potential ethical concerns.

Data privacy: ChatGPT requires access to personal data, such as user conversations and information, to provide personalized learning support. However, there is a potential risk that this data may be utilized for unintended purposes, such as profiling or targeted advertising, making it crucial to protect users' data privacy and ensure that it is used only for intended purposes.

Bias and discrimination: The model used by ChatGPT is trained on large datasets, which may contain biased or discriminatory information. As a result, the model may generate biased or discriminatory responses. It is essential to monitor and address any possible biases in both the training data and model output to ensure that ChatGPT provides fair and unbiased support.

Dependency: Students may develop an excessive dependence on ChatGPT for learning support, which could result in a lack of self-directed learning and critical thinking abilities. It is important to recognize ChatGPT as a learning support tool, rather than a substitute for active engagement and independent thinking.

Lack of personal interaction: Although ChatGPT can provide on-demand support, it cannot replace the benefits of personal interaction with teachers, tutors, and peers. As a result, students should be provided with opportunities for personal interaction and collaboration to support their learning and social development.

> **ChatGPT is a game-changing learning assistant that offers a wide range of benefits to students. Its adaptability, efficiency, accessibility, and convenience make it an excellent resource for students of all ages and learning styles. However, it is important to remember that technology can never replace human teachers or mentors. Instead, ChatGPT should be seen as a valuable tool that can supplement and enhance the learning experience, providing students with personalized support and guidance to help them reach their full potential.**

Developing 21st-Century Skills with ChatGPT: The Way Forward

As we move deeper into the 21st century, the 4Cs (creativity, critical thinking, communication, and collaboration) have become increasingly essential for success in the modern workforce. However, with the continuous development of artificial intelligence (AI) technology such as ChatGPT, it has become clear that these skills must evolve to prepare students for a future that involves working with AI systems. While AI can provide a wealth of information and assist with various tasks, it is not yet a substitute for human skills and knowledge. To ensure that students are prepared for the opportunities and challenges that come with AI, what changes are necessary for the 4Cs and what additional skills must students develop?

Evolving the 4Cs with ChatGPT

Critical thinking: While AI can process vast amounts of information quickly, it may not be able to analyze it in the same way that humans can. It is essential for educators to teach students how to ask thoughtful questions, identify biases, and analyze information in a way that AI cannot. For instance, students can be given a project where they must analyze a complex problem such as climate change. They can use ChatGPT to gather data and insights, but they must apply critical thinking to evaluate the data and draw conclusions based on the evidence. This way, students can develop the ability to analyze complex information and make informed decisions.

Creativity: In a world where AI can generate ideas and suggestions, students must learn to develop these AI generated ideas into creative and innovative solutions. This involves challenging students to take an AI-generated idea and develop it further, making it unique and personalized to their own circumstances. For example, students could be challenged to come up with solutions to their own problems, such as finding ways to exercise more regularly. While ChatGPT could provide ideas such as setting achievable goals or finding an enjoyable exercise, students must be able to take these ideas and develop them in a way that is feasible and effective for their own situation. This requires students to sharpen their creativity and come up with new, innovative approaches to problem-solving that go beyond what AI can offer.

Communication: In addition to effective communication with humans, students must learn how to communicate with ChatGPT in a way that maximizes its potential. This includes asking ChatGPT the right questions to get the most helpful responses, providing context and feedback to help ChatGPT improve, and evaluating the quality and accuracy of the information provided. For practice, students can be given exercises that involve interacting with ChatGPT to develop their communication skills, such as asking it to summarize complex concepts, explain difficult topics, or provide feedback on their writing.

Collaboration: While ChatGPT can provide information and assistance, it may not be able to promote collaboration and teamwork in the same way that humans can. However, with the increasing use of online collaboration tools and communication platforms, students must learn how to work with ChatGPT as a member of their team. For example, they can use ChatGPT as an "assistant" to help them research and develop their ideas, and then collaborate with their peers to refine and implement their plans. Working with ChatGPT and each other, students can enhance their collaboration and achieve their goals.

Other core skills for the world with ChatGPT

Emotional intelligence: This is an essential skill that goes beyond just managing one's own emotions. Students must also learn how to empathize and understand the emotional states of others, including AI systems like ChatGPT. Since AI lacks emotions, students can be taught how to build healthy and meaningful relationships with AI, such as by acknowledging its limitations and appreciating the unique ways in which it can contribute to their learning and work. By fostering emotional intelligence, students can develop a more respectful approach to working with AI.

Adaptability: With the rapid pace of AI technology evolution, students will need to learn how to stay up to date with new developments and be adaptable in their approach to learning and problem-solving. Educators can help students develop a growth mindset, emphasizing adaptability, flexibility, and continuous learning. To do this, students can be given projects where they must use emerging technologies like ChatGPT to solve complex problems. With a growth mindset and the ability to learn and apply new technology effectively, students can become more adaptable and prepared for the changing demands of the modern workforce.

Digital literacy: With the increasing prevalence of AI in various industries, it has become essential for students to learn how to interact with and use technology effectively. This includes knowing how to use various AI tools and software and how to integrate them into their work. Students should be given hands-on projects where they can apply AI tools to generate data or solve problems. For instance, students can be assigned a project where they must use ChatGPT to generate possible solutions. They can also be taught how to critically evaluate the quality of the AI-generated results and interpret them in their own context. Equipped with digital literacy, students can use AI tools effectively and efficiently.

Ethics and responsibility: As AI technology becomes more advanced and influential in society, it is critical that students understand the ethical and social implications of working with AI. Educators can teach students about responsible AI use, including topics like privacy, security, and fairness, as well as potential biases in the data that ChatGPT may use to generate responses. For instance, students can be given ethical issues related to AI and asked to debate their solutions, taking into consideration the potential impact on individuals and society as a whole. This ethical awareness and responsibility can help students ensure that they use ChatGPT and other AI tools in a responsible and respectful manner.

As AI technology continues to advance and become more integrated into our lives, it is crucial for students to develop a range of skills that prepare them for working alongside AI systems like ChatGPT. As the famous computer scientist Alan Kay once said, "The best way to predict the future is to invent it." Preparing students to work alongside AI, we are helping to invent a future in which these systems can be used to their full potential to benefit the society.

Maximizing ChatGPT's Benefits: Tips for Students

Are you looking for a powerful tool to enhance your learning experience and improve your creativity as a student? Look no further than ChatGPT, a sophisticated language model that can provide answers to a wide range of questions and engage in conversations on a variety of topics.

With ChatGPT, students can conduct research, boost creativity, find entertainment, and explore personal development goals. Let's explore some practical ideas for students to make the most of ChatGPT's capabilities and take their learning journey to the next level. Students can unlock a range of benefits, including access to a vast database of information, learning skills development, and even opportunities for entertainment and socializing. Whether you're looking for a way to improve your research skills, enhance your creativity, or find some entertainment in between study sessions, ChatGPT has something to offer.

ChatGPT for research

ChatGPT's ability to provide students with quick access to relevant and reliable information for research. ChatGPT can understand natural language and generate responses based on its massive knowledge base, which makes it an excellent tool for answering research questions. For instance, students can ask ChatGPT for an explanation of a complex concept, a historical event, or a scientific theory. ChatGPT can also provide references and links to credible sources for further research.

Examples of research questions that can be answered using ChatGPT:

- *What are the major causes of global warming?*

- *How did the Civil Rights Movement impact the United States?*

- *What is the difference between a virus and a bacterium?*

Tips:

- Use clear and concise language when asking questions.
- Verify the information provided by ChatGPT with additional sources.
- Use ChatGPT's responses as a starting point for further research.

ChatGPT for learning

ChatGPT can be an excellent tool for students who want to enhance their learning experience. With its massive knowledge, ChatGPT can help students understand complex concepts and ideas. For example, students can use ChatGPT to get an explanation of a particular topic, practice a foreign language, or get homework help.

Examples of learning topics that can be explored using ChatGPT:

- *What is the Pythagorean theorem, and how is it used?*
- *How do you conjugate irregular verbs in Spanish?*
- *What is the difference between a sonnet and a haiku?*

Tips:

- Ask open-ended questions to encourage conversation and exploration.
- Use ChatGPT's responses as a way to supplement your learning materials.
- Ask for clarification if you don't understand a response.

ChatGPT for writing

ChatGPT serves as a beneficial resource for students seeking to enhance their writing abilities. With its ability to generate innovative ideas, offer constructive feedback, and propose helpful revisions, ChatGPT can assist students in cultivating their writing skills with greater confidence and creativity.

Practical ideas for using ChatGPT for writing:

- Ask ChatGPT for writing prompts, brainstorming ideas, or inspiration on a specific topic.

- Ask ChatGPT for feedback on writing samples and suggestions for improvement.
- Ask ChatGPT to generate text in different writing styles and genres, providing students with inspiration and ideas for experimenting with their own writing style.

Tips:

- Use clear and concise language when asking ChatGPT for assistance.
- Verify any information generated by ChatGPT with additional sources to ensure accuracy.
- Use ChatGPT's responses as a way to gain inspiration and motivation for writing.

ChatGPT for creativity

Using ChatGPT can inspire students to explore their creative side. With ChatGPT's assistance, students can unleash their creativity and initiate exciting new projects. Whether they need writing prompts, brainstorming assistance, or innovative product concepts, ChatGPT can help them achieve their goals.

Examples of creative projects that can be started with ChatGPT's help:

- Write a short story based on the prompt "a world without technology."
- Brainstorm ideas for a new product that solves a common problem.
- Come up with a design of a special means of transport.

Tips:

- Use ChatGPT to generate ideas that you can build upon.
- Don't be afraid to experiment and try new things.
- Use ChatGPT's responses as a way to spark your imagination.

LE · Let's Come up with a design of a special means of transport.

Sure, I'd love to help! Let's brainstorm some ideas for a special means of transport.

1. Flying Car: A vehicle that can transform into a small airplane and take off vertically. It would be able to land and take off from anywhere and would have a high degree of maneuverability. It could be used for personal transportation, as well as emergency services and search and rescue operations.
2. Personal Rapid Transit: A network of small, automated vehicles that transport people directly to their destination. These vehicles would run on a dedicated track, allowing them to move quickly and efficiently without the need for stops. They would be ideal for

ChatGPT for entertainment

Interacting with ChatGPT can provide a source of amusement for students. By participating in enjoyable activities with ChatGPT, students can temporarily disconnect from their studies and enjoy themselves. Students have the option of engaging in games, sharing humor, or conversing with ChatGPT for entertainment.

Some fun activities that can be done with ChatGPT:

- Play a game of "20 Questions" with ChatGPT.
- Ask ChatGPT to tell you a joke or a riddle.
- Have a conversation with ChatGPT about a favorite topic.

Tips:

- Be creative and open-minded when interacting with ChatGPT.
- Don't take things too seriously and have fun.
- Use ChatGPT as a way to unwind and relax.

LE · Let's play 20 questions

Sure, I'd be happy to play 20 Questions with you! You can start by asking the first question.

LE · Is it an animal?

Alright, I've got your first question. The answer is: Yes, it is an animal. That leaves you with 19 more questions to narrow it down. What's your second question?

ChatGPT for personal growth

Utilizing ChatGPT can aid in the personal growth of students. Through questioning oneself and examining personal aspirations, students can attain invaluable perspectives and gain clarity about their lives. For example, ChatGPT can assist students in establishing objectives, cultivating mindfulness, and discovering novel interests.

Examples of personal growth goals that can be achieved with ChatGPT:

- Set a goal for personal growth and ask ChatGPT for advice on how to achieve it.

- Practice mindfulness meditation with the help of ChatGPT.

- Learn a new hobby or skill by asking ChatGPT for guidance.

Tips:

- Use ChatGPT to generate ideas that you can build upon.

- Don't be afraid to experiment and try new things.

- Use ChatGPT's responses as a way to spark your imagination.

In the current era of technology, students have an abundance of resources and tools at their disposal to assist them in achieving their objectives and realizing their maximum potential. Among the various options available, ChatGPT stands out as an exceptionally versatile and potent tool, providing students with numerous advantages. Hence, it is recommended to give ChatGPT a try and encourage students to explore its multiple benefits that can enhance both their academic and personal growth.

Chapter III: ChatGPT and Teaching

Unlocking Student Insights with ChatGPT

Effective teaching requires a deep understanding of students' perspectives, making it crucial for educators to gather and analyze data on their students. Consequently, educators must collect and scrutinize data on their students to achieve this understanding, a process that can be arduous and time-consuming. This is where ChatGPT shines, showcasing its ability to aid teachers in obtaining a more profound insight into their students by analyzing data, making the process more efficient and effective.

Benefits of using ChatGPT for analyzing student data

Analyzing student data with ChatGPT can provide valuable insights into student learning patterns and progress, allowing teachers to personalize their instruction and improve student outcomes.

One of the key benefits of analyzing student data with ChatGPT is that it allows teachers to see and understand student learning patterns that they may not have been able to see otherwise. If a teacher notices that a student is struggling with a particular concept, they may ask ChatGPT to analyze the student's writing and identify common mistakes or areas where they could improve. This can help the teacher to tailor their instruction to meet the student's needs, providing targeted support and resources to help them succeed.

Another benefit is that it can help teachers to personalize their teaching approach for individual students. Gaining insights into a student's writing style, vocabulary, or sentence structure, for example, helps the teacher create customized learning activities that specifically target areas where the student needs help. This can increase engagement and motivation, as students are more likely to be interested in and engaged with the material that is tailored to their needs and interests.

Analyzing student data can also help teachers track student progress over time. By analyzing patterns in student test scores, writing samples, and other data, teachers can identify areas where students are improving or struggling and adjust their instruction accordingly. This can help to ensure that all students are making progress and achieving their learning goals.

In addition, analyzing student data assists teachers in identifying areas where they may need to adjust their teaching methods or curriculum. For example, if a teacher notices that many students are struggling with a particular concept, they may need to modify their approach to better meet the needs of the class. With insights into student learning patterns and progress, teachers can make informed decisions about how to improve their teaching and help students to succeed.

The process to use ChatGPT for analyzing student data

When it comes to analyzing student data using ChatGPT, there are a few important steps to keep in mind.

The first step is to collect and organize the data in a format that can be processed by the tool. One common approach is to use a learning management system (LMS) that can track student progress and generate reports based on their performance. This can include data such as test scores, writing samples, and other relevant information.

Once the data has been collected and organized, the next step is to input it into ChatGPT and prompt it to provide insights based on specific criteria. Depending on the platform or software being used, teachers can input data into ChatGPT using a variety of methods, such as uploading a file, copy-pasting text, or typing a natural language prompt such as "analyze the vocabulary used in this student's writing sample" or "identify patterns in this student's test scores."

After receiving the input, ChatGPT processes the data using natural language processing (NLP) algorithms. It can recognize patterns and relationships in the data and generate insights in the form of summaries, visualizations, or written reports.

Once the data has been processed and insights provided, teachers can review the results to gain a better understanding of student learning patterns and tailor their instruction accordingly.

To provide a specific example, let's say a teacher wants to understand a particular student's reading comprehension. They might input the student's latest reading assessment into ChatGPT and prompt it to analyze the student's understanding of the main idea. ChatGPT could then provide insights into the main idea and supporting details the student identified, as well as any gaps or misunderstandings they might have had. The teacher could use this information to adjust their lesson plans and teaching strategies to address the student's specific needs, such as focusing on building better comprehension skills or providing additional support with identifying key details.

Some more examples of how ChatGPT can help teachers gain insights into students' needs and learning patterns.

- **Analyzing quiz responses:** ChatGPT can be used to analyze student responses to quizzes or surveys. It can identify which questions students struggled with the most, helping the teacher to better understand where their students need more support.

- **Writing analysis:** Students' writing can be analyzed by ChatGPT in terms of their writing style, vocabulary, sentence structure, and grammar. It can identify common mistakes that students make and provide suggestions for improvement.

- **Engagement analysis:** ChatGPT can analyze student engagement with course material, such as how often they participate in class discussions or how much time they spend on homework assignments. This information can help teachers identify students who may need extra support or motivation.

- **Language proficiency analysis:** Student's language proficiency can also be analyzed. ChatGTP can examine their writing or speaking samples (by transcribing and examining the student's speech). It can provide insights into their vocabulary range, grammatical accuracy, and overall proficiency level and suggest appropriate teaching strategies to improve their language skills.

- **Sentiment analysis:** ChatGPT can analyze the sentiment of student writing or feedback to understand their emotional state or level of engagement. With this, teachers can identify when students may be struggling or disengaged, and support appropriately.

Best practices for using ChatGPT to analyze student data

To ensure that teachers are using ChatGPT ethically and effectively, there are some best practices that they should follow despite the tool's potential to provide valuable insights into student performance.

First, teachers must be careful to protect student privacy and ensure that they are using the data in a responsible and ethical way. This might involve obtaining consent from students and their parents, or working with school administrators to establish clear policies around data collection and use.

Second, while the tool is capable of generating human-like responses, it is not perfect and may make errors or misinterpret data. Teachers should therefore be cautious when interpreting insights generated by ChatGPT and consider other sources of data to validate its findings.

Third, teachers should use ChatGPT as one tool among many for analyzing student data. While it can provide valuable insights, it is important to also consider other factors that may be impacting student performance, such as outside factors like family or health issues.

Fourth, teachers should use the insights gained from ChatGPT to inform their teaching approach and make adjustments as needed. This might involve creating customized learning activities for individual students, providing additional support or resources for struggling students, or modifying teaching methods to better align with student learning styles.

ChatGPT is an advanced tool that empowers teachers to gain a deeper understanding of their students' insights by analyzing various data sets. By leveraging ChatGPT's analytical capabilities, educators can obtain valuable insights into their students' learning patterns and requirements, which can enable them to adjust their teaching practices accordingly to better support their learners. While there are challenges and limitations associated with utilizing ChatGPT for student data analysis, the potential benefits of this technology make it an essential tool for educators to explore.

From Good to Great: How ChatGPT Enhances Lesson Planning

As teachers, our goal is to craft compelling and impactful lesson plans that facilitate the learning and development of our students. Nevertheless, devising fresh and captivating approaches that accommodate diverse learning styles and aptitudes can be challenging. That's where ChatGPT comes into play - an AI-based learning algorithm that can propose innovative lesson concepts, recommend structural frameworks, and provide interactive activities and games to foster student engagement and participation.

How ChatGPT suggests customized lesson ideas and activities

ChatGPT can suggest lesson ideas and activities by analyzing a variety of sources, including textbooks, research articles, and educational websites. Teachers only need to input the learning objectives and topic of the lesson, and ChatGPT can generate a range of lesson ideas and activities that are tailored to the specific needs of the students. For example, if a teacher is planning a lesson on environmental conservation, ChatGPT could suggest a range of activities such as creating a recycled art project, conducting a sustainability audit of the school, or researching and presenting on a particular environmental issue.

ChatGPT can also propose lesson planning and ideas based on student learning style and needs. ChatGPT has the ability to analyze and understand different learning styles and needs of students, based on which it can provide valuable suggestions and recommendations to teachers for creating more personalized and effective lesson plans. If a teacher is planning a lesson on a specific topic, ChatGPT can analyze the learning style of each student in the class and suggest appropriate teaching strategies. To illustrate, if most students in class learn better through visual aids, ChatGPT might recommend using more visual elements such as diagrams, images, and videos to convey the information.

In terms of time-efficiency, using ChatGPT to generate lesson ideas can be a real time-saver for teachers. As Hieu Nguyen, a high school English teacher in Ho Chi Minh City, explains, "With ChatGPT, I can quickly get ideas for my lesson plans without having to spend hours researching different sources. It's really helpful to have a tool that can generate relevant and personalized ideas based on my specific learning objectives and topic."

How ChatGPT provides guidance on lesson structure and learning experiences

In addition to suggesting lesson ideas and activities, ChatGPT can provide guidance on structuring lessons and creating effective learning experiences for students. For instance, ChatGPT might suggest starting the lesson with a clear introduction that explains the learning objectives and provides context for the topic.

ChatGPT can also offer guidance on creating engaging activities that help students achieve learning outcomes. This might include suggesting interactive exercises, group activities, or real-world examples that illustrate the relevance of the topic. If a teacher wants to create an interactive exercise to reinforce a concept, ChatGPT can provide suggestions for activities that will make the learning experience more engaging for students. Similarly, if a teacher wants to incorporate group work to encourage collaboration, ChatGPT can suggest where (in which part of the lesson) to organize a group-work activity.

Utilizing ChatGPT to guide lesson structure and learning experiences can assist teachers in creating more effective lessons that help their students achieve the desired learning outcomes. ChatGPT has the ability to help teachers think more critically about how they structure their lessons, ensuring the lessons are engaging, effective, and relevant to their students' needs.

How ChatGPT suggests interactive activities and games

One of the most valuable features of ChatGPT is its ability to suggest interactive activities and games that keep students engaged and motivated during class. For example, ChatGPT might suggest a math game that challenges students to solve problems using fractions, which can help to make the learning experience more engaging and enjoyable.

Similarly, ChatGPT could recommend a sentence scramble game that encourages students to practice a specific language grammar point.

By incorporating these interactive elements into their lessons, teachers can help students stay focused on and increase retention of the material. As Julie Hoffman, a fifth-grade teacher at an international primary school in Vietnam, notes, "Using ChatGPT to find interactive activities has really helped me engage my students. They love the games and exercises, and it's made my lessons much more enjoyable for everyone."

Concerns of using ChatGPT for creating engaging lesson plans

While ChatGPT offers many advantanges for teachers looking to create engaging and effective lesson plans, there are also some concerns that may arise when using this technology. One concern is that ChatGPT may not always provide accurate or appropriate suggestions. Since ChatGPT is a machine learning algorithm, it may not have the same level of understanding and contextual knowledge as a human teacher. This means that it is crucial for teachers to review and assess the suggestions made by ChatGPT to ensure that they align with their students' learning needs and abilities.

Another concern is that relying too heavily on ChatGPT may limit a teacher's creativity and flexibility in lesson planning. While ChatGPT can provide guidance and ideas, teachers also need to incorporate their own expertise and experience into their lesson plans. Teachers should use ChatGPT as a tool to supplement their own ideas and creativity, rather than as a replacement for it.

It can be said that ChatGPT has transformed the way teachers approach lesson planning and create meaningful learning experiences for their students. With its cutting-edge machine learning algorithms, ChatGPT provides tailored suggestions for activities and ideas, which teachers can use to design lessons optimized to their students' unique learning styles and abilities. As technology continues to evolve, it is likely that more educators will adopt tools like ChatGPT to enhance their teaching capabilities and deliver exceptional educational outcomes.

ChatGPT: The Key to Reducing Teacher Workload

Teaching is a demanding profession that requires a significant investment of time and effort from teachers. From lesson planning and grading to communicating with students and identifying those who need additional support, teachers have a lot on their plate. These challenges can lead to stress and burnout, making it difficult for teachers to provide the best possible education for their students. Fortunately, there's a new tool that can help: ChatGPT.

ChatGPT is an advanced language model developed by OpenAI that can assist teachers in various tasks, including generating lesson plans, providing personalized feedback to students, automating grading, and answering common student questions. But how exactly can ChatGPT help reduce teachers' workload, and what are the benefits of using it?

The challenges of teacher workload

Teaching is a multifaceted profession that requires a wide range of skills and knowledge, and their working days do not end when the final school bell rings. Teachers are responsible for planning lessons that align with curriculum standards and meet the needs of diverse learners, grading assignments and tests, communicating with students and parents, and identifying those who need additional support. However, these tasks can be time-consuming and overwhelming, particularly for teachers who are already stretched thin.

According to a recent survey conducted by the EdWeek Research Center, a typical teacher works about 54 hours a week—with just under half of that time devoted to directly teaching students. That means on average, a teacher spends more than 25 hours per week on work-related tasks, including grading, lesson planning, and communicating with students and parents, etc. This workload can lead to burnout and decreased effectiveness in the classroom, as teachers may not have enough time and energy to focus on individual student needs and provide personalized feedback and support.

How ChatGPT can reduce teacher workload

Generating lesson plans: One of the most time-consuming tasks for teachers is creating lesson plans, especially the ones that meet the needs of all learners. ChatGPT can help by generating personalized lesson plans based on student data, such as their learning styles, strengths, and weaknesses. If a teacher inputs information about a student's preferred learning style, ChatGPT can generate lesson plans that incorporate visual aids, hands-on activities, or other methods that align with that student's needs.

Providing personalized feedback to students: Another difficulty that teachers often face is providing personalized feedback to students on their assignments and tests. However, with the help of ChatGPT, this task can become more manageable. ChatGPT can generate feedback that is specifically tailored to each student's strengths and weaknesses. For instance, if a student has difficulty with grammar, ChatGPT can offer targeted feedback on their writing that emphasizes grammar errors and provides useful suggestions for improvement.

Automating grading of assignments and tests: Teachers often find grading assignments and tests to be a time-consuming task, especially when dealing with large classes. To tackle this challenge, there are two ways for teachers to grade their students' work with ChatGPT's assistance. They can either put the answers in ChatGPT manually, or they can integrate ChatGPT with an online platform or learning management system where students have already submitted their answers. ChatGPT can then automate the grading process and provide students with prompt feedback, which can help to save teachers' time and enhance the learning experience.

Answering common student questions: Teachers are often occupied with answering repetitive and common student queries, such as "What chapter should I read for tomorrow?" or "What time is the assignment due?". To automate the response to repetitive queries, teachers can input frequently asked questions and corresponding answers into ChatGPT's system. With ChatGPT addressing such routine questions, teachers can focus on handling more critical tasks, such as providing individualized support to students who need it the most. Utilizing ChatGPT for this, teachers can also promote a more efficient and effective learning environment for students.

Identifying struggling students for interventions: Identifying struggling students can be another challenge for teachers, especially in larger classes. ChatGPT can assist in this job by analyzing student data, such as grades and attendance records. ChatGPT can then suggest interventions and support strategies that align with the student's needs. This ensures that struggling students receive the support they need to succeed, while also reducing the workload for teachers.

Advantages of employing ChatGPT to minimize teacher workload

Reducing teachers' workload with the assistance of ChatGPT can have several benefits for teachers, students, and the education system as a whole.

First, ChatGPT's ability to automate repetitive and time-consuming tasks can help reduce the workload of teachers and decrease their stress and burnout levels. This can have a positive impact on their mental health and well-being, allowing them to be more engaged, motivated, and effective in the classroom and provide better support to their students.

Second, with ChatGPT handling tasks like grading and answering common student questions, teachers can have more time and energy to focus on teaching and engaging with their students. This can lead to more effective teaching and learning experiences, as teachers can provide individualized support and feedback to each student.

Third, by generating personalized feedback, lesson plans, and targeted support for struggling students, ChatGPT can help improve student outcomes. Students are more likely to succeed when they receive personalized support that meets their unique needs and learning styles, and thanks to ChatGPT teachers can provide that support more efficiently.

Fourth, professional development is an essential component of a teacher's career growth. By reducing the workload, ChatGPT enables teachers to invest more time and effort into their professional development. They can participate in training programs, attend workshops, and engage in research activities to enhance their teaching skills and knowledge, hopefully leading to better learning outcomes.

Last but certainly not least, reducing the workload of teachers can have a positive impact on building a quality teaching community. With reduced tasks done by ChatGPT, teachers can focus more on collaboration and sharing best practices with their colleagues, creating a supportive and collaborative teaching community where teachers can learn from one another, share resources, and support each other in their professional growth.

Challenges and considerations

While ChatGPT has the potential to reduce teachers' workload and improve student outcomes, there are also some challenges and considerations to keep in mind when implementing this technology.

When using ChatGPT to assist teachers, it is crucial to ensure the privacy and security of student data. Teachers should take appropriate measures to safeguard student information and comply with all applicable privacy and security regulations. By doing so, they can help create a safe and secure learning environment for their students and build trust with parents and other stakeholders.

Another challenge when using ChatGPT is ensuring that the content generated aligns with curriculum standards and teaching philosophies. Teachers should review all ChatGPT-generated content and make any necessary edits or revisions to ensure that it meets their standards and aligns with their teaching goals and objectives. This may require some additional time and effort, but it can help ensure that the content generated by ChatGPT is useful and effective in supporting student learning.

While ChatGPT can assist teachers in various tasks, it is important to ensure that it does not replace the role of the teacher in providing human connection and support. Teachers should use ChatGPT as a tool to enhance their teaching and provide additional support, rather than relying on it as a substitute for human interaction.

ChatGPT can be a game-changer for teachers to reduce their administrative workload, allowing them to focus on student engagement and targeted support. While the potential benefits are substantial, it is important to consider the challenges and best practices for implementing ChatGPT effectively. With careful consideration, ChatGPT can assist teachers in enhancing teaching and improving student outcomes.

Reference

https://www.edweek.org/teaching-learning/how-teachers-spend-their-time-a-breakdown/2022/04. Accessed 9 March, 2023.

ChatGPT: The Missing Link in Teacher Professional Development

Teachers hold a crucial responsibility as educators in shaping the future of society. Their job entails more than just imparting knowledge and skills; it also involves instilling in students positive values, attitudes, and goals. To be effective, however, teachers require continuous professional development (PD) to stay abreast of the latest research and best practices in their field. ChatGPT aims to bridge this gap by providing personalized and adaptive learning opportunities that tackle the challenges of time and resource constraints, lack of personalization, staying current, and tackling irrelevant or impractical learning topics.

Explicit challenges of teacher PD

Teachers often have limited time and resources to engage in PD, as they are juggling multiple responsibilities, such as teaching, planning, grading, and administrative tasks. Moreover, not all schools or districts have the budget or infrastructure to provide PD opportunities.

Traditional PD models often offer a one-size-fits-all approach, which may not meet the unique needs and preferences of individual teachers. Some teachers may prefer self-paced learning, while others may prefer interactive or collaborative learning. Some may learn better with face-to-face workshops, while others may be more beneficial with webinars.

With the fast pace of technological advancements and changes in education policy and practice, teachers may find it challenging to stay up-to-date with the latest research and trends in their field. This can make it difficult for teachers to effectively use new tools and methodologies in the classroom and provide the best possible education for their students.

Some PD opportunities may not be realistic or relevant to teachers' classroom needs, which can lead to frustration, disengagement, and a waste of time and resources. For example, a teacher who teaches in a low-income school may not benefit from a PD on using expensive technology tools or resources.

How ChatGPT supports teacher PD

Schools are always concerned about the effectiveness of teacher PD due to the difficulties that come with it. However, with the emergence of AI tools such as ChatGPT, there is hope that these concerns can be addressed in some way.

Helping teachers stay updated with the latest research and trends: With ChatGPT's assistance, teachers can stay updated with the latest research and trends in their field by providing access to up-to-date information and insights. This can be particularly useful in rapidly evolving fields, such as educational technology. Besides, ChatGPT can summarize complex information and provide relevant examples or applications, making it easier for teachers to understand and apply the knowledge.

Increasing time for teacher PD: ChatGPT can increase time for teacher PD by automating administrative tasks and providing efficient solutions to common problems such as scheduling, grading, or lesson planning, freeing up teachers' time to engage in PD activities. Donovan, an English teacher at an ELT center, said, "Instead of spending hours grading papers, I can now use ChatGPT to provide instant feedback to my students, which frees up more time for me to participate in PD activities the school offers."

Suggesting a variety of relevant PD resources: ChatGPT can suggest a variety of relevant PD resources, including articles, webinars, podcasts, and courses. These resources can be personalized based on teachers' needs, interests, and learning preferences, and can best fit the teachers' classroom problems. "I was struggling with how to differentiate instruction for my diverse learners. ChaTGPT provided me with several articles and videos that explain different strategies and tools for differentiation. It saved me a lot of time and effort, and I was able to apply some of the ideas in my classroom right away," a Maths teacher at a secondary school expressed.

Providing personalized and adaptive learning opportunities: ChatGPT is capable of offering personalized and adaptive learning opportunities that cater to the unique needs, interests, and learning preferences of teachers. By leveraging its advanced capabilities, ChatGPT can help teachers identify their strengths and weaknesses, as well as their goals and interests, to create a tailored learning plan that meets their specific requirements. For example, if a teacher wishes to enhance their questioning skills, ChatGPT can propose a customized plan that includes relevant resources, activities, and feedback to support them in achieving their goal. As teachers make progress and provide feedback, the plan can be adjusted over time to ensure that the learning experience remains engaging and relevant.

Providing real-time feedback and support during classroom teaching: ChatGPT can provide real-time feedback and support to teachers during their classroom teaching. Teachers can use ChatGPT to ask for help, advice, or feedback, and receive immediate responses that can help them make better decisions and improve student learning outcomes. "ChatGPT has been a lifesaver for me in class! It's given me real-time feedback and support, so I can totally cater to my students' needs and tweak my teaching strategies on the fly," said a teacher at a STEM extracurricular school.

Concerns of utilizing ChatGPT in teacher PD

While ChatGPT has many benefits for teacher PD, it is not without its potential challenges and limitations. Some of the most notable concerns are privacy and security, potential biases and inaccuracies in responses, and the need for human interaction and support.

Privacy and security concerns are always a top priority when using any online platform, especially when it involves sensitive information like personal and PD. Teachers need to be aware of the platform's privacy policy and take appropriate measures to protect their data. ChatGPT has a robust security and privacy policy in place to ensure users' data is kept confidential and secure. However, it is always recommended that teachers exercise caution and remain vigilant when sharing personal or professional information online.

Another potential limitation of ChatGPT is the potential for biases and inaccuracies in responses. While ChatGPT is trained on vast amounts of data, it is still a machine learning algorithm and can have limitations in understanding context and nuance. Therefore, teachers should always approach ChatGPT responses with a critical and analytical mind, and not rely solely on its suggestions.

Despite the fact that ChatGPT can provide personalized and adaptive learning opportunities, it cannot replace human interaction and support. Teachers still need to have access to mentors, coaches, and colleagues for feedback, support, and collaboration. ChatGPT can be used as a supplement to traditional PD opportunities, but it should not be viewed as a replacement.

ChatGPT can serve as a missing link in teacher PD by addressing various common challenges they encounter. It can function as a potent tool to help teachers improve their knowledge, skills, and confidence, resulting in improved student outcomes. Despite some potential limitations and challenges that need consideration, teachers should embrace the opportunities that ChatGPT offers and utilize its capabilities to enhance their professional growth and impact.

Making the Most of ChatGPT: Tips for Teachers

In today's modern life, technology plays a significant role, and educators are constantly seeking new ways to incorporate it into their teaching practices. One such innovative tool is ChatGPT, a language model that can generate human-like responses to text-based prompts. With its capacity to provide instant feedback and support, teachers can utilize ChatGPT to enhance their teaching practices and support their students' learning. However, it is essential to explore how ChatGPT can be integrated into the classroom and beyond. What are some practical ideas for teachers to use ChatGPT both in and outside of the classroom?

Using ChatGPT in the classroom

Creating engaging classroom discussions with ChatGPT: ChatGPT can be used to create engaging classroom discussions by generating questions or prompts for students to respond to. A teacher can use ChatGPT to generate a question or a debatable scenario related to a topic they are covering in class, such as an ethical dilemma or a scientific hypothesis, and ask students to consider different perspectives and potential outcomes. This can help students develop their critical thinking and analytical skills, while also promoting a collaborative and interactive classroom environment and encouraging active participation from all students.

Incorporating ChatGPT in group projects and presentations: Teachers can assign students to incorporate ChatGPT into group projects or presentations. Students can use ChatGPT to generate content or research topics related to their projects, and then present their findings to the class. Another example is to use it as a writing assistant. ChatGPT can assist by generating outlines or drafts for written assignments, and then revising and editing the output to create a polished final product. Utilizing ChatGPT in this way can encourage students to think critically, creatively, and engage with their projects in a more meaningful way.

Using ChatGPT to answer student questions in real-time: One of the key benefits of using ChatGPT in the classroom is the ability to answer student questions in real-time. When students have questions about a particular topic or concept, with ChatGPT, teachers can provide feedback and support instantly. Teachers can also have ChatGPT generate answers to frequently asked questions related to a topic they are teaching and provide them to students during class or in a separate Q&A session. This approach can help students feel more engaged and connected to the material, as they are getting the information they need in real-time.

Providing personalized feedback to students using ChatGPT: ChatGPT's ability to generate human-like responses to text-based prompts can be used to provide personalized feedback to students on their work or assignments. For instance, a teacher can upload a student's written assignment to ChatGPT, which will then evaluate the student's writing and provide feedback on areas that need improvement. This approach to feedback is particularly beneficial because it allows teachers to provide targeted and specific feedback to each student. This, in turn, can help students to better understand their areas of strength and areas for improvement, enhancing student engagement and motivation and leading to more efficient learning.

Using ChatGPT to evaluate student understanding and knowledge retention: When it comes to assessing student understanding and knowledge retention, ChatGPT can generate questions or quizzes related to a topic that students have recently learned. Using ChatGPT for this purpose, teachers can assess student understanding and knowledge retention in a way that is both efficient and effective. The model can generate a large number of questions in a short amount of time, enabling teachers to assess a wide range of topics and concepts. Additionally, with the questions generated by an AI model, they are less likely to be biased or influenced by personal opinions or preferences.

Using ChatGPT-generated quizzes and games: Using ChatGPT to create quizzes and games is a great way to personalize learning experiences for students. ChatGPT can generate questions related to a current topic and create a quiz or a game that students can play as a class or individually. For instance, if a high school science teacher wishes to create a quiz on the human body, he can ask ChatGPT to create a game with questions that cover different aspects of the topic, from identifying different organs in the body to understanding how the digestive system works. This approach offers a fun and interactive way for students to review and reinforce their learning, while also providing teachers with a way to assess student understanding.

Using ChatGPT beyond the classroom

Assigning ChatGPT as a research tool for homework and projects: This is a powerful way to encourage independent research and critical thinking skills in students. Teachers can assign students to use ChatGPT to research a particular topic or question, and then present their findings in class. For example, in a history class, a teacher can assign students to use ChatGPT to research a particular historical figure or event, and then present their findings to the class. This can be a useful way to encourage independent research and critical thinking skills.

Encouraging students to use ChatGPT for self-directed learning: Encouraging students to take charge of their own learning is an important part of any effective education system. ChatGPT can be a right tool for promoting self-directed learning outside of the classroom, as students can use it to generate questions and explore topics that interest them. A student who is fascinated by astronomy, for example, can use ChatGPT to generate questions related to the subject, such as "What are black holes?" or "How do stars form?" Armed with these questions, the student can then research and learn more about the topic on their own, using a variety of resources to deepen their understanding. By promoting self-directed learning in this way, teachers allow students to pursue their own interests and passions, fostering a love of learning that will serve students well throughout their lives.

Offering study guides and review materials: ChatGPT can help teachers create study guides and review materials for students to use outside of class time. Imagine that a teacher wants to create a set of flashcards or a quiz to help students review key terms or concepts from a recent lesson. Instead of spending hours creating these materials themselves, the teacher could input the relevant terms or concepts into ChatGPT and ask it to generate a quiz or flashcards. ChatGPT will then generate a set of questions or flashcards based on the inputs. These materials can be shared with students through a learning management system (LMS) or other digital platform, allowing them to review and study at their own pace.

Generating lesson ideas and activities: Generating ideas for lesson plans and classroom activities is an essential part of lesson planning for teachers. With ChatGPT, teachers can streamline this process and generate ideas for their lessons in the blink of an eye. For instance, a teacher who is planning a lesson on climate change can input this topic into ChatGPT and receive a list of related ideas, such as the causes of climate change, its effects on the environment, and possible solutions to combat it. Using ChatGPT in this way can save teachers time and energy, as they can quickly generate new ideas for their lessons without having to spend hours researching and developing their own ideas.

Using ChatGPT for professional development: One way to use ChatGPT for professional development is to use it as a research tool. ChatGPT can help teachers quickly and easily find information on a topic of interest, allowing them to stay informed and up-to-date. For example, if a teacher is interested in learning more about the latest teaching strategies for teaching math to elementary students, he can use ChatGPT to search for articles, blog posts, and other resources on this topic. Another way to improve professionally with ChatGPT is using it as a tool for self-reflection. A teacher might ask ChatGPT a question such as "What are some effective strategies for promoting student engagement in the classroom?" He can then reflect on ChatGPT's responses and consider how they might incorporate them into their own teaching practices.

As technology continues to transform the way we live and work, it is essential for educators to explore new ways to integrate it into their teaching practices. ChatGPT is a magic tool that can help teachers create engaging and personalized learning experiences for their students, both inside and outside of the classroom. From generating questions for classroom discussions to providing personalized feedback on student work, ChatGPT can enhance the learning experience and promote student success, and it is up to educators to embrace and utilize it to create the best possible learning experiences for their students.

Chapter IV: ChatGPT and the Changing Face of Education

The Role of ChatGPT in Modernizing School Operations

Modern schools encounter an array of challenges, such as managing administrative tasks, ensuring student safety, and delivering high-quality education. Fortunately, recent advancements in Artificial Intelligence (AI) have introduced an innovative solution to enhance school operations and streamline processes: ChatGPT. As an AI-powered chatbot, ChatGPT can automate tasks, provide support, and answer inquiries, making it an invaluable tool for schools. With its potential to transform school operations, let's explore the benefits of ChatGPT, how to implement it effectively, and the future of this technology in education.

Benefits of ChatGPT in school operations

Streamlining administrative tasks: Administrative tasks can take up a significant amount of time and resources for school staff. ChatGPT can help by automating tasks such as scheduling meetings, sending reminders, and managing attendance. This frees up staff to focus on more complex tasks. For instance, ChatGPT can manage student enrollment, allowing parents to complete the process quickly and efficiently. The chatbot can ask for necessary documents, verify information, and even provide updates on the enrollment status. With this, parents can complete the enrollment process without the need for staff intervention.

Facilitating communication: Effective communication is essential in any organization, and schools are no exception. ChatGPT can help by providing an instant response to student and parent inquiries, saving time and reducing wait times. ChatGPT chatbot can answer common questions such as school policies, schedules, and events. The chatbot can also provide personalized support for students by recommending resources such as study materials or tutoring services. This helps not only to improve student engagement and academic performance but to save time and resources for the school as well.

Optimizing teaching staff efficiency: By utilizing ChatGPT's automated feedback system based on student performance, school staff can optimize their efficiency. The chatbot can analyze responses from quizzes, assignments, and exams to identify areas where students excel or require improvement. As a result, school staff can save time and effort that would otherwise be spent on grading and providing feedback and focus on other academic tasks and operations, enhancing their overall productivity.

Improving school safety: Safety is a top priority for schools, and ChatGPT can help by providing emergency support and monitoring student behavior. For example, ChatGPT can monitor students' conversations and detect any concerning language or behavior. If a student were to use language that suggests they are feeling depressed or suicidal, ChatGPT could flag this as a potential risk and notify school administrators or counselors to intervene and provide support. In addition, ChatGPT can be programmed to provide emergency support to students or staff members in need such as giving guidance on how to respond and directing them to the appropriate resources for help.

Common pitfalls and ethical considerations

As with any new technology, there are always pitfalls and ethical considerations to keep in mind when implementing ChatGPT in schools. Below are some of the key issues to consider.

Users' potential objections: One of the common pitfalls of implementing ChatGPT in schools is addressing common concerns and potential objections from parents and students regarding the use of AI technology. Some may feel uncomfortable with the idea of a machine handling personal information and interacting with students. Therefore, schools must address these concerns by providing clear and transparent information about how ChatGPT works, what data is collected, and how it is used. This will help build trust and ensure that parents and students feel comfortable using the chatbot.

Bias and fairness: Implementing ChatGPT comes along with the risk of bias and unfairness in the chatbot's responses. Chatbots learn from the data they are trained on, which means that they may pick up biases or inaccuracies that are present in the data. To prevent bias and ensure fairness, schools should take steps to carefully select and curate the data used to train the chatbot. This can include selecting data from a diverse range of sources and ensuring that the data is representative of the school's student body. Schools can also program the chatbot to avoid sensitive or controversial topics that could lead to biased or inaccurate responses.

Monitoring and supervising ChatGPT: While the chatbot is designed to operate independently, it is still important to monitor its performance and ensure that it is providing unbiased, accurate, and appropriate responses. Schools should assign a designated staff member or team to oversee the chatbot's performance, monitor its interactions with users, and identify any areas where it may need additional training or updates. The chatbot needs this support so that it can operate effectively and provide a positive user experience. Moreover, having a designated point of contact for issues related to the chatbot can help to streamline communication and ensure that any problems are addressed quickly and efficiently.

Lack of emotional intelligence :Another potential pitfall of ChatGPT is its lack of emotional intelligence. While the chatbot is designed to provide accurate and informative responses, it may not be able to understand or respond appropriately to emotional or nuanced situations. For example, if a student is experiencing a mental health crisis or emotional distress, the chatbot may not be equipped to provide the level of support and guidance that a trained professional could provide. To address this pitfall, schools should clearly communicate the limitations of ChatGPT to students and parents. Schools can also consider incorporating additional tools or resources to supplement the chatbot's responses, such as online mental health resources or hotlines for students to call.

ChatGPT is a highly beneficial tool that can greatly improve school operations and streamline various processes, which can assist schools in achieving their objectives more efficiently. However, successful implementation of ChatGPT requires careful planning and training.

As AI technology continues to advance, ChatGPT's value as an asset for schools will continue to grow. Its capabilities to help schools improve their operations and provide students with a better learning experience are significant, and its potential to support schools will become even more critical in the future.

Enhancing School Efficiency and Productivity with ChatGPT

In today's fast-paced world, where time is a valuable commodity, productivity and efficiency are critical for success in any sector. The education sector is no exception, and schools are continually seeking new ways to enhance productivity and efficiency to ensure that students receive the best possible education. To achieve this, schools are turning to artificial intelligence (AI) solutions, and one of the most powerful AI tools available today is ChatGPT. As an advanced language model trained by OpenAI, ChatGPT can help enhance productivity and efficiency in school settings and why these improvements are crucial for student success.

How ChatGPT improves productivity

Improving communication: Effective communication is crucial in schools, and ChatGPT can help improve communication between teachers, students, and administrators. ChatGPT can help answer student queries and provide assistance to students who need help. This allows teachers and admin staff to focus on more important tasks such as lesson planning and student engagement. Thanks to ChatGPT, administrators can also communicate more effectively with teachers and students, streamlining workflows and reducing response times.

Providing valuable insights: ChatGPT can help the school with valuable insights into student learning. By analyzing data from assessments and other sources, ChatGPT can identify areas where students are struggling and provide recommendations on how to improve student performance. Moreover, as ChatGPT is capable of tracking student progress over time, the school can identify trends and patterns in student learning and have interventions when necessary.

Streamlining workflows: ChatGPT can help streamline workflows in schools, making processes more efficient and reducing errors. For example, admin staff can use ChatGPT to automate the process of scheduling parent-teacher conferences or setting up meetings between teachers and administrators. This reduces the amount of time and effort required to complete these tasks, allowing staff to focus on more critical tasks.

Enhancing student assessments: ChatGPT can be used to improve the quality of student assessments. Teachers can create assessments that are tailored to students' individual learning needs, which can help improve student performance. ChatGPT can analyze data from previous assessments and provide insights into the types of questions that students find challenging, helping teachers create more effective assessments. Another benefit is ChatGPT's ability to provide personalized feedback to students, helping them identify areas where they need to improve and providing suggestions on how to do so.

How ChatGPT improves efficiency

Identifying areas of inefficiency: ChatGPT is a powerful AI tool that can help schools identify areas of inefficiency and optimize workflows to enhance productivity. ChatGPT can analyze data from various sources and provide valuable insights into school operations, enabling administrators to pinpoint bottlenecks and take steps to optimize schedules and resources. This, in turn, can lead to better matching of teachers' skills with tasks, as well as optimizing classrooms for student learning. For instance, ChatGPT can detect when a teacher is spending too much time on administrative tasks, leaving less time for lesson planning. School administrators can then take corrective action by reassigning those tasks to another staff member or automating them, thereby freeing up the teacher's time for lesson planning.

Automating repetitive tasks: ChatGPT's capability to automate repetitive tasks can save valuable time and effort for teachers. For instance, grading assignments can be a time-consuming process, especially when dealing with a large number of students. With ChatGPT, teachers can automate the grading process, freeing up more time to focus on other important tasks. This not only saves time but also ensures consistency in grading across all assignments. ChatGPT can also be used to automate other repetitive tasks such as data entry, lesson planning, and scheduling.

Providing support for teachers and students: For students, ChatGPT can provide instant feedback on assignments, helping them identify areas where they need to improve and providing suggestions for how they can do so. This can be particularly helpful for students who are struggling in certain subjects or who need extra support. Rather than having to wait for a teacher to grade an assignment and provide feedback, students can receive immediate guidance from ChatGPT. This not only helps students improve their performance but can help them build their confidence and motivation as well.

For teachers, ChatGPT can assist with lesson planning by offering suggestions for activities and resources that match the needs of their students. For instance, if a teacher is planning a lesson on a particular topic, ChatGPT can suggest relevant videos, articles, or interactive activities that the teacher can incorporate into their lesson plan. Besides lesson planning, grading and giving feedback, creating assignments, and assigning homework are also tasks that ChatGPT can help with among others. All of these can help teachers save time and ensure that they are providing engaging and effective learning experiences for their students.

Potential drawbacks and limitations

While ChatGPT offers many potential benefits to schools, it is essential to consider potential drawbacks and limitations. One of the major concerns is the accuracy of ChatGPT's responses, which are dependent on the quality of the data it has been trained on. If the data is biased or inaccurate, ChatGPT's responses may also be biased or inaccurate, which could have a negative impact on student learning outcomes.

Another concern is privacy and data security, especially when using ChatGPT to store student data. Schools must ensure that they have robust security measures in place to protect student data and that they comply with data privacy regulations.

Finally, it is important to recognize that ChatGPT cannot substitute the human element in education entirely. While ChatGPT can help automate tasks and provide assistance, it cannot replace the valuable experience and insight that teachers bring to the table. Teachers play a critical role in student learning and development, and they must remain at the center of the educational process.

> **ChatGPT can actually make an enormous impact on the education sector. Its advanced capabilities can transform the way schools operate, significantly enhancing productivity and efficiency. It cannot be denied that ChatGPT is a must-have tool for any school that is serious about enhancing productivity and efficiency, and providing students with the best possible learning experience. It can place the schools ahead of the curve so that they can deliver high-quality education.**

ChatGPT: A Catalyst for Equity and Inclusivity in Education

As society becomes increasingly diverse, educators and policy makers face the challenge of ensuring that every student has an equal opportunity to learn and succeed. Educational equity and inclusivity are two key concepts that can help address this challenge. Educational equity means that every student has access to the resources and opportunities they need to succeed, regardless of their race, ethnicity, gender, socioeconomic status, or other factors. Inclusivity means that every student feels valued and respected, and that their cultural background and identity are acknowledged and celebrated. Now that ChatGPT has appeared and become a magic tool in every aspect of education, let's explore how it is making education more equitable and inclusive.

Understanding educational equity and inclusivity

Before finding how ChatGPT can promote educational equity and inclusivity, it is necessary for us to look at what these concepts mean among academia and why they are so important in education.

Educational equity is the idea of "creating an educational system that caters to students of all kinds and develops their educational experience accordingly" (WGU, 2021) so that every student should have access to the resources and opportunities they need to succeed, regardless of their background or identity. Educational equity is different from equality, which is simply providing everyone with the same resources and opportunities. Equity, on the other hand, recognizes that some students may need more support and resources to overcome their disadvantages if any. This includes access to high-quality instruction, support services, and resources such as textbooks, technology, and other learning tools. In an equitable educational environment, every student is given the support and resources they need to succeed, and they are not held back by barriers such as poverty, discrimination, or disability.

Educational inclusivity is defined as "an on-going process aimed at offering quality education for all while respecting diversity and the different needs and abilities, characteristics and learning expectations of the students and communities, eliminating all forms of discrimination" (UNESCO, 2009, p.126). That is the idea that every student should feel valued and respected, and that their cultural background and identity are acknowledged and celebrated. This includes creating an environment where all students feel comfortable expressing their opinions and sharing their experiences, and where diversity is seen as a strength rather than a weakness. In an inclusive classroom, students are encouraged to express themselves and their cultural identities, and their unique perspectives and experiences are respected and celebrated. Inclusivity also means creating policies and practices that ensure that all students have equal opportunities to participate in classroom activities and discussions, and that they are not excluded or marginalized by their instructor or peers.

Equity and inclusivity are essential in education because they help to create a more fair and just education system. They ensure that every student, regardless of their background or abilities, has access to high-quality education and is given the support and resources they need to succeed. Embracing equity and inclusion, schools and educators can create a more diverse and inclusive learning environment that prepares students to live and work in a multicultural world. Furthermore, education equity and inclusivity can help to reduce disparities in educational outcomes and create more opportunities for all students to reach their full potential.

"The principles of inclusion and equity are not only about ensuring access to education, but also about having quality learning spaces and pedagogies that enable students to thrive, to understand their realities, and to work for a more just society." (UNESCO, 2017, p.18)

Promoting educational equity with ChatGPT

First, ChatGPT provides access to information that might otherwise be unavailable to students. For example, ChatGPT can answer questions on a wide range of subjects, including science, math, history, and more. This means that students in rural or low-income areas who might not have access to a physical library or other resources can still access the information they need to succeed in their studies.

Second, ChatGPT assists with personalized learning that can cater to the needs of students with varying learning styles and interests. ChatGPT can adjust its responses to assist students who may find it challenging to learn in a conventional classroom setting, or suggest personalized learning resources to each student to enhance their engagement in the learning process. This approach can provide equitable opportunities for students who may have limited access to educational resources.

Third, ChatGPT supports diverse learning styles by offering a range of tools and resources that cater to students' individual learning preferences. For visual learners, ChatGPT can recommend audio or visual aids. It can also provide interactive simulations or games for students who prefer hands-on learning. These features help to ensure that all students, regardless of their learning style, have an equitable opportunity to learn and succeed.

Fourth, ChatGPT can provide support for students with special needs. Students who have visual impairments can take advantage of ChatGPT's text-to-speech capabilities, enabling them to listen to the text instead of reading it. This feature can help them to access information and complete their coursework independently. Similarly, students with hearing impairments can use ChatGPT's speech recognition technology to type in their responses and participate in class discussions, which can help them to feel more included in the learning process.

Promoting educational inclusivity with ChatGPT

Inclusivity is another key component in modern education, and ChatGPT can play an important role in creating a more inclusive learning environment. One way it does this is by providing language support and translation services. ChatGPT can translate content into multiple languages, which can help students who are non-native speakers of the language of instruction to better understand the material. This can help to reduce language barriers and ensure that every student has an equal opportunity to learn and participate in the classroom.

Another way ChatGPT promotes inclusivity is by providing a safe and non-judgmental space for students to ask questions and seek help. Students who are hesitant to ask questions or seek help in a traditional classroom environment for fear of being judged or stigmatized can feel more comfortable approaching ChatGPT for assistance. This can help to increase engagement and participation among students who might otherwise be reluctant to engage in classroom discussions.

ChatGPT can also help promote culturally responsive teaching practices by providing educators with resources and lesson plans that incorporate diverse perspectives and experiences. For instance, ChatGPT can provide recommendations for books, articles, and other resources that feature diverse characters and authors, or that explore topics related to diversity and inclusion. Incorporating these resources into their curriculum helps educators to create a more inclusive and culturally responsive learning environment.

Functioning as a platform to share their experiences and perspectives is another way ChatGPT promotes inclusivity in the classroom. Students can use ChatGPT to ask questions about different cultures and traditions, or to share their own experiences and perspectives with their peers. This can help create a more open and inclusive learning environment, where students feel valued and respected for their unique perspectives, identities, and backgrounds.

Challenges for consideration

While ChatGPT has shown promising results in promoting educational equity and inclusivity, it also faces certain challenges and limitations that need to be addressed to ensure its effectiveness.

ChatGPT is a machine learning model that is trained on large datasets of text, which it uses to generate responses to user input. However, the quality of its responses depends on the quality of the data it has been trained on. If the training data contains biases or incomplete information, these biases may be replicated by ChatGPT and perpetuated in its responses. For example, if the training data predominantly includes examples of certain demographics or cultural backgrounds, ChatGPT may be more likely to provide responses that are tailored to these groups and not be as effective for others. This can lead to perpetuating inequities in education and reinforcing existing biases and stereotypes.

The cultural sensitivity of ChatGPT is a significant challenge that needs to be addressed to ensure that it can effectively support all students, regardless of their cultural background. Culture plays a crucial role in shaping how individuals communicate, learn, and process information, and ChatGPT's programming may not be aligned with certain cultural norms and values. To illustrate, some cultures prioritize collective learning and collaboration, whereas others emphasize individual learning and self-reliance. Moreover, some cultures may view direct criticism or negative feedback as disrespectful or inappropriate, while others may view it as necessary for improvement. These cultural differences may affect how students communicate with ChatGPT and how they interpret its responses.

These challenges highlight the importance of curating and training ChatGPT with diverse and inclusive datasets to ensure that it can effectively promote educational equity and inclusivity. This involves training ChatGPT with data that represents diverse cultural backgrounds, socioeconomic statuses, and learning abilities, as well as incorporating culturally relevant examples and perspectives into its training data. Educators and developers of ChatGPT can also work with diverse student groups and cultural experts to identify and address potential biases and ensure that ChatGPT is culturally sensitive and appropriate for all students. These steps can help ensure that ChatGPT is an effective tool for promoting educational equity and inclusivity.

Overall, the potential of ChatGPT to promote educational equity and inclusivity is immense, and it is up to educators and policy makers to support its use and development. Recognizing the importance of equity and inclusivity in education, and embracing innovative technologies like ChatGPT will ensure that all students have the support and resources they need to achieve their full potential in their studies.

References

UNESCO (2017). *A Guide for Ensuring Inclusion and Equity in Education.* Paris: United Nations Educational, Scientific and Cultural Organization. https://unesdoc.unesco.org/ark:/48223/pf0000248254. Accessed 13 March, 2023.

UNESCO (2009). Defining an Inclusive Education Agenda: Reflections around the 48th session of the International Conference on Education. UNESCO. http://www.ibe.unesco.org/sites/default/files/resources/defining_inclusiv e_education_agenda_2009.pdf. Accessed 13 March, 2023.

WGU (2021). *An Overview of Equity in Education.*

https://www.wgu.edu/blog/overview-equity-education2107.html#close. Accessed 13 March, 2023.

ChatGPT's Power in the Non-Traditional Learning Environments

In recent years, especially during and after the COVID-19 pandemic, non-traditional learning such as online learning, remote learning, and homeschooling have become increasingly popular in the education sector. These types of learning offer greater flexibility and accessibility, allowing students to study at their own pace and from any location. On the other hand, they also come with their own set of challenges, such as lack of personalization and interactivity, difficulty in tracking progress, and limited access to resources. Fortunately, there is a promising solution that can address these challenges and enhance learning outcomes: ChatGPT.

Online Learning, Remote Learning, and Homeschooling

Online learning refers to a type of education that is delivered via the Internet, allowing students to study from any location with an internet connection. In this format, students typically engage with a teacher who is teaching the class through an online learning platform such as Zoom or Google Meet.

Remote learning, on the other hand, is a broader term that refers to any type of education that is delivered to students who are physically separated from the teacher or institution providing the instruction. This can take various forms, such as video conferencing, live-streamed lectures, or pre-recorded videos.

Homeschooling is a form of education where parents or guardians take on the responsibility of teaching their children at home, usually using a structured curriculum. This differs from traditional schooling where the responsibility of educating children is primarily taken on by a school and its teachers. With the blooming of online learning during the pandemic, homeschoolers may choose to supplement their curriculum with online classes or tutoring sessions taught by a teacher via an online learning platform. This allows them to access resources and expertise beyond what is available through their own curriculum.

The challenges

These types of learning have gained popularity for their accessibility and flexibility, but they also come with challenges. One of the main challenges is lack of personalization and interactivity. In traditional classroom settings, teachers can tailor instruction to students' needs, abilities, and interests, and engage students in interactive discussions and activities. When learning at home, students may have limited interaction with teachers and peers, and may receive generic or non-adaptive instruction, which can impact their learning outcomes and engagement.

Tracking students' progress and providing timely feedback is also a concern. In traditional classrooms, teachers can easily monitor students' progress through various methods such as assessments, observations, and feedback. On the contrary, in non-traditional learning environments, tracking progress can be more difficult due to several reasons. It is because first, students may be scattered across different locations, time zones, or even countries like in an online learning class. Second, it is because students may not have regular face-to-face interactions with teachers and peers. Without regular face-to-face interactions, it may be challenging for teachers to observe students and give promptly feedback to identify any areas where students may be struggling or falling behind.

The next challenge is related to limited access to resources. This means that the students may not have access to the types of educational resources that are typically available in traditional educational settings such as textbooks, libraries, and labs. Students may have to rely solely on digital resources, which may not always be reliable or of high quality. For example, they may encounter outdated or inaccurate information on the Internet, or they may not have access to the latest research in their field of study. This difficulty may hinder students from acquiring the knowledge and skills they need to succeed in their chosen field.

When ChatGPT comes in...

As an AI-powered conversational agent that can converse with students in natural language, ChatGPT can provide personalized instruction and feedback. This feature makes it an ideal tool to address the above mentioned challenges and enhance learning outcomes in online learning, remote learning, and homeschooling. Below are some ways that ChatGPT can enhance these types of non-traditional learning.

Personalization and adaptability: ChatGPT can provide personalized learning experiences to individual students, adapting to their unique learning styles, abilities, and interests. Students can provide prompts to ChatGPT, such as questions, statements, or essays, and receive customized responses that address their specific needs. It can also adjust the level of difficulty, provide additional explanations or examples, and track progress, ensuring that students receive the right amount and type of instruction.

Interactivity and engagement: ChatGPT can engage students in interactive conversations, making learning more interesting and fun. Students can discuss with ChatGPT to share ideas, ask questions, and receive feedback from ChatGPT. Communication and collaboration among students can be facilitated by ChatGPT, too, allowing them to work together on projects, share resources, and learn from each other.

Accessibility and flexibility: With ChatGPT, education can become more accessible for students with disabilities, as well as students who may not have access to traditional educational resources. Students with visual impairments can use chat-based interfaces with ChatGPT to access educational content, and students in remote or underserved areas can access ChatGPT-powered education from anywhere with an internet connection. ChatGPT can also offer flexible learning options, such as asynchronous learning, that accommodate students' schedules and lifestyles.

Monitoring progress and offering feedback: ChatGPT has the capability to collect data on a learner's performance on various assessments, quizzes, and surveys, allowing for effective tracking of their progress. This data can then be used to provide timely feedback to learners, which can prove to be highly valuable in helping them adjust their study habits and improve their performance. In addition, ChatGPT's constructive feedback can highlight areas where a learner may be struggling, and suggest specific ways to overcome those difficulties.

Access to resources: ChatGPT offers a vast array of educational resources, including textbooks, articles, and multimedia content, which are tailored to students' individual interests and needs. By leveraging ChatGPT's recommendations, students can quickly and easily locate the information they require to excel in their studies. These resources enable students to deepen their comprehension and expertise in specific subjects, as well as to broaden their skill set.

ChatGPT, as an advanced language model, can contribute significantly to improving the quality and accessibility of non-traditional forms of education, such as online learning, remote learning, and homeschooling. However, it is crucial to ensure that everyone has access to the necessary technology and infrastructure to take advantage of this tool. Efforts, therefore, must be made to ensure that all students, regardless of their socio-economic status, have access to the necessary technology to engage in non-traditional education effectively.

The Promise and Perils of Intergrating ChatGPT in Education

ChatGPT is an AI language model that is capable of generating responses to natural language inputs that are virtually indistinguishable from those of human beings. This technology has already been utilized in various domains, such as chatbots, virtual assistants, and customer service applications. Within the field of education, ChatGPT holds promise for significantly improving the quality of teaching and learning, but its integration comes with several notable obstacles, including technical limitations, ethical considerations, policy gaps, and pedagogical challenges.

Challenges of implementing ChatGPT in education

Technical limitations:

Despite its impressive capabilities, ChatGPT has technical limitations that need to be addressed to ensure its effective use in education. One of the most significant limitations is the quality and quantity of training data that ChatGPT is exposed to. In order to operate effectively, ChatGPT is trained on vast quantities of text data, and while this approach has proven highly effective in many contexts, there is a risk that it may be biased and not fully representative of educational content. As a result, the accuracy of ChatGPT's responses may be limited and not specific to educational settings.

The next issue is technology accessibility. Specifically, in many remote or low-income areas, students and educators may not have access to the necessary technology infrastructure to support the use of ChatGPT in the classroom. This may include a lack of reliable internet connectivity, limited access to computing devices, or insufficient technical support for implementing and maintaining the system. Without adequate access to these resources, the potential benefits of ChatGPT in education may be limited to only certain groups of students or regions, perpetuating existing inequities and inequalities in education.

Ethical considerations:

One of the most significant ethical considerations surrounding the use of ChatGPT in education is the risk to data privacy and security. ChatGPT requires the processing of enormous amounts of data, which may contain sensitive information about students and teachers. Such data may include personal identifiers, academic records, and other sensitive information. If this data falls into the wrong hands, it can lead to significant privacy violations and negative consequences for the affected individuals.

ChatGPT's impact on social and emotional learning is another ethical concern. While ChatGPT may provide assistance to students, it may not be able to replicate the same level of emotional support and empathy as a human teacher. This may impact a student's social and emotional development, leading to negative consequences in their overall academic progress and personal growth.

The risk of using ChatGPT to cheat is one serious ethical issue. Students may use the technology to bypass learning activities, resulting in their inability to develop necessary academic skills. This concern could undermine the entire educational system, as it poses a significant challenge to the legitimacy of assessment practices and overall learning outcomes.

Policy gaps:

The lack of well-defined policies and guidelines for implementing ChatGPT in education presents a notable challenge. Effective and ethical use of ChatGPT requires a clear framework of policies and guidelines that address issues such as data privacy and security, student-teacher interactions, and academic integrity. However, due to the rapid pace of technological advancements, the policy landscape regarding ChatGPT is still evolving, and as such, there is a pressing need for policymakers to work towards developing clear policies and guidelines that will ensure the ethical and effective use of ChatGPT in education.

Such policies and guidelines should take into account the diverse needs and contexts of different educational settings and ensure that the use of ChatGPT aligns with the principles of responsible and equitable technology use. In the absence of such policies, the widespread adoption of ChatGPT in education could lead to unintended consequences such as student exploitation, privacy violations, or academic dishonesty.

Pedagogical challenges:

Integrating ChatGPT in education presents a host of pedagogical challenges. One key obstacle is ensuring that the AI-generated responses align with the curriculum and educational goals. For ChatGPT to be a useful tool in education, its responses must be directly relevant to the educational content and support the achievement of learning objectives. To this end, teachers will need to be trained in how to utilize ChatGPT effectively within their curriculum.

Another obstacle is that ChatGPT may have a negative impact on students' critical thinking skills and creativity. By providing students with ready-made answers without requiring them to engage in the thinking process, ChatGPT may potentially stunt the development of these crucial cognitive abilities. Thus, it will be vital for educators to be mindful of the appropriate ways to integrate ChatGPT into the classroom, such that it augments, rather than replaces, students' own problem-solving processes.

The next challenge is training teachers to incorporate ChatGPT effectively into their teaching practices. Given that this technology is still relatively new and developing rapidly, educators will need ongoing professional development opportunities to stay up-to-date with best practices for integrating ChatGPT in the classroom. This training should include instruction on how to use ChatGPT in ways that align with learning objectives and support critical thinking, as well as how to ensure that the technology is used ethically and appropriately.

Actions for implementing ChatGPT in education

To successfully integrate ChatGPT in education, a number of actions need to be taken to address the challenges and mitigate potential risks.

Below are some recommended steps that policymakers, educators, and technology developers can take.

Develop clear policies and guidelines:

Developing clear policies and guidelines for the integration of ChatGPT in education is crucial to ensure that the technology is used in an ethical and effective manner. Policies should be established to address issues such as data privacy and security, ensuring that student and teacher data is protected when using ChatGPT. Policies should also outline the appropriate use of the technology in the classroom, such as when and how ChatGPT can be used to support learning or assessment.

In addition, appropriate guidelines need to be developed to support teachers in utilizing ChatGPT in their teaching. For example, guidelines should specify that ChatGPT cannot be used to replace human interaction. While ChatGPT has the ability to interact with students and provide valuable feedback, it is vital to remember that the chatbot is still a machine and cannot replace the human connection that is essential to effective teaching and learning.

To prevent students from using ChatGPT to cheat on exams, policies and guidelines should clearly mention how teachers and parents should monitor students' device usage during exams or how teachers create exams that require more than simple memorization or basic comprehension.

Invest in teacher professional development:

This is a critical action to successfully integrate ChatGPT into the curriculum. Many teachers may not have experience with AI language models like ChatGPT. Providing teachers with professional development programs they need to use ChatGPT effectively can help them to unlock its potential to enhance learning outcomes.

These professional development programs for teachers can take many forms. One approach is to provide teachers with hands-on training sessions where they can experiment with using ChatGPT in different classroom scenarios. Another approach is to offer online courses or webinars that focus on the pedagogical aspects of using ChatGPT in the classroom. In addition, on-the-job training, mentoring, coaching, and sharing sessions are other forms of professional development.

For the effective integration of ChatGPT into education, it is essential to provide teachers with proper training and support. Without this, it is impossible to envision a successful implementation.

Foster critical and creative thinking:

Fostering critical and creative thinking skills in students ensures that ChatGPT enhances learning outcomes rather than simply providing students with quick answers. Teachers can achieve this by developing their own critical thinking skills and teaching students how to use ChatGPT to foster theirs, which enable students to form judgments and make decisions based on evidence, rather than relying on preconceptions or emotions.

One way teachers can foster critical and creative thinking skills is by asking open-ended questions that require more than a simple factual answer, or asking them to solve a complex problem such as climate change. For instance, instead of asking students what the temperature is in New York City, teachers can ask a more creative question, such as "What would be the impacts of an increase in temperature in New York City over the next 50 years?" This type of question requires students to use ChatGPT wisely and judge its responses critically and creatively. This not only helps students to have a deep understanding of learning concepts, but also can lead to the habit of always thinking carefully about the information provided by ChatGPT before using it.

With fostered critical and creative thinking skills, teachers and students can ensure that ChatGPT is used in a way that promotes deeper learning and critical analysis, rather than simply providing quick and easy answers or solutions to their problems.

Address technology divide:

With the integration of ChatGPT in education, equitable access to technology and internet connectivity is more critical than ever. Without these resources, students will not be able to access the benefits of ChatGPT-powered learning tools. Policymakers can address this issue by investing in the necessary infrastructure to support technology and internet connectivity in schools and communities. This may include funding for upgrading or building new computer labs or technology centers, providing high-speed internet access to underserved areas, and ensuring that students have access to devices such as laptops, tablets, or smartphones.

In some cases, schools may also need to provide students with internet hotspots or other mobile devices to ensure that they can access ChatGPT. This is particularly important for students who may not have access to technology or Internet at home due to financial or geographical barriers. Schools can also cooperate with technology companies or device suppliers to provide discounts so that more students can have adequate access to ChatGPT.

Promote ethical and responsible use of technology:

As a powerful tool, ChatGPT can be tempting for students to use it for cheating or to rely too heavily on it. Teachers must educate students on the proper use of ChatGPT and help them to develop a clear understanding of the ethical considerations involved in using the technology.

One example of ethical use of ChatGPT is its use in research. Students can use ChatGPT to gather information for their research, but they must ensure that they use the technology responsibly and give proper credit to the sources they use. Teachers must provide guidance and ensure that students understand the importance of citing sources properly.

Teachers must also promote ethical and responsible use of technology in general. This includes educating students on the potential risks associated with using technology, such as cyberbullying, online harassment, and identity theft. By promoting ethical and responsible use of technology, teachers can help students to develop the skills and understanding necessary to navigate the digital world safely and responsibly.

While ChatGPT offers immense potential to revolutionize the way teaching and learning is done, its integration also poses significant challenges that cannot be overlooked. To effectively address these challenges, it is essential for policymakers, educators, and technology developers to work together in a coordinated manner. By doing so, we can ensure that ChatGPT is used ethically and effectively to enhance learning outcomes for all students. Only through such collaborative efforts can we harness the full potential of this technology and usher in a new era of education.

As Ahmed Belhoul Al Falasi, the Minister of Education in the UAE, aptly stated in the World Government Summit 2023, "The onus right now is on us…to catch up with developing technology, to fully use AI, to be trained on how to use it and then make students write their own version of what they have learnt."

Reference

https://www.edarabia.com/uae-minister-education-gives-speech-fully-written-chatgpt. Accessed 17 March, 2023.

Chapter V: Tips and Strategies for Using ChatGPT

Dispelling the Top 7 Myths About ChatGPT

ChatGPT, developed by OpenAI, is a language model that has the ability to generate human-like responses to a wide range of prompts. Its advanced capabilities have led to a growing interest in using ChatGPT for various applications, from customer service and content creation to research and education. However, despite its impressive abilities, there are still many myths and misunderstandings about ChatGPT that can lead to incorrect expectations and limitations on its use. So, what are the top 7 myths about ChatGPT?

Myth #1: ChatGPT is a human

One of the biggest misconceptions about ChatGPT is that it is considered a human. Although ChatGPT can generate responses that seem as if they are written by a person, this is far from the truth. ChatGPT is an AI model that uses complex algorithms and machine learning to generate responses to questions and prompts. It is trained on a massive corpus of text data, allowing it to produce human-like responses, but it is important to remember that it is simply a computer program and not a human.

Myth #2: ChatGPT has personal opinions

ChatGPT is programmed to respond based on the information it was trained on, and it does not have personal opinions. The responses it generates are a result of its programming, not personal beliefs or biases. For example, when asked about that product, ChatGPT may generate positive responses. However, it is simply because the information it was trained on contained positive comments about the product; it is not ChatGPT's personal opinion about that product.

Myth #3: ChatGPT can replace human interaction

ChatGPT is an excellent tool for generating text and answering questions, but it cannot replace human interaction. While ChatGPT can assist with answering questions and generating text, it cannot replace the emotional intelligence and interpersonal skills that humans possess. Moreover, it may not always understand the nuances of human language or the context of a conversation. For instance, ChatGPT may be able to respond to customer service inquiries, but it cannot replace the empathy and personalized attention that a human customer service representative can provide.

Myth #4: ChatGPT is always accurate

ChatGPT generates responses based on the information it was trained on. Therefore, the accuracy of the responses depends on that of the training data. Hence, it can still make mistakes. Also, ChatGPT can be manipulated by adversarial examples or biased training data, and the model's outputs can reflect these biases or manipulations. While it is highly advanced, it is important to critically evaluate the accuracy of ChatGPT's responses before using or relying on them.

Myth #5: ChatGPT can solve all problems

ChatGPT can assist with generating text and answering questions, but it is not capable of solving all problems. It is a tool, not a solution. While ChatGPT may be able to assist with troubleshooting a technical issue, it may not be able to completely resolve the problem. So, it is important for us to use it as a tool to support problem-solving, rather than relying on it to solve all problems.

Myth #6: ChatGPT can develop emotions, empathy, and creativity

ChatGPT has been trained on text data and can generate text-based responses. It does not have the ability to experience emotions, empathy, or creativity in the same way as a human. While it may generate responses that appear emotional or creative, it is because it has been trained on text data that includes expressions that express emotions and creativity.

It does not reflect a true emotional or creative experience. For example, ChatGPT may respond to your sad feeling or event with an expression of sympathy, but it definitely does not have the ability to truly feel empathy or sadness.

Myth #7: ChatGPT can perform complex tasks on its own

While ChatGPT can generate code snippets or technical writing, it does not have the ability to perform complex coding or engineering tasks on its own such as executing the code, debugging it, or building a software system from scratch without human intervention. Also, it is not capable of designing, building, or testing complex software systems, and requires human intervention to perform these tasks. In other words, despite advancements, ChatGPT still requires human expertise to perform complex tasks.

ChatGPT is a powerful AI model that has the potential to transform the way we communicate and solve problems. While it is capable of generating human-like responses, it is important to understand that it is not perfect and can be limited. By dispelling the myths about ChatGPT and understanding its true nature, we can better utilize its capabilities to support and augment human communication and problem-solving, and by using it wisely, we can unlock its full potential.

ChatGPT: The 6 Benefits for Students

As technology continues to shape the way we teach and learn, ChatGPT, an advanced language model developed by OpenAI, presents a unique opportunity for English language teachers to revolutionize their classrooms. With its ability to generate human-like text, ChatGPT can be integrated into various aspects of language teaching, making it a valuable tool for enhancing student engagement, facilitating effective communication and promoting critical thinking. Let's explore how ChatGPT can enhance the learning experience for English language students and revolutionize the way English is taught in the classroom.

Improving writing skills

One of the primary benefits of ChatGPT is its ability to help students improve their writing skills. With the model's writing prompt functionality, teachers can prompt students to write on a specific topic or genre, and receive feedback on their work in real-time. This not only saves time but also ensures that students receive personalized feedback, which can help them identify and correct their writing mistakes.

For instance, a teacher can prompt students to write a descriptive paragraph about their favorite place and ask ChatGPT to generate feedback. This could include comments such as "Great use of descriptive language! However, try to add more details about the sounds and smells of the place to make it more vivid for the reader." This type of feedback helps students to improve their writing skills by giving them specific suggestions for improvement.

Can you help with 2 main feedback on my student's writing below?
Danang is a beautiful city in central Vietnam. Having tropical climate, Danang is hot and wet all the year. Danang is famous of tourism. It has Ba Na Hill on the top of mountains. In central city, there are many bridges. The most famous bridge is Han River, the country's first swing bridge and Dragon Bridge. Danang has many beautiful beaches and caves. This city also has many traditional cuisine that make foreigners praise and remember. This is the most worth-living city m Vietnam according to fore gn newspapers.

Sure, here are two main pieces of feedback for your student's writing: 

1. Clarity and Sentence Structure:

The student's writing is relatively clear, but some sentences are quite short and simple, making the writing seem choppy and disjointed. Encourage your student to vary the sentence structure by combining shorter sentences or using transitional words and phrases to connect ideas.

For example, the first two sentences could be combined to create a more complex sentence: "Danang, a beautiful city in central Vietnam, has a tropical climate that makes it hot and wet year-round."

Improving speaking skills

In addition to improving writing skills, ChatGPT can be used as a language tool to help students improve their speaking skills. The human-like text generated by ChatGPT will be used to facilitate conversations between students, allowing them to practice their speaking skills in a natural and engaging way.

For example, a teacher can create a conversation between two students, with ChatGPT playing the role of one of the students. The teacher can then use the generated text to facilitate conversation between the students, where they will be able to practice their speaking skills with each other. In this way, ChatGPT helps to create an environment for students to practice their speaking skills, not a direct conversational partner. This not only promotes speaking skills but also helps students build confidence in speaking English.

Facilitating effective communication

Another advantage of using ChatGPT in the classroom is that it can facilitate effective communication between students. With its ability to understand and generate human-like text, ChatGPT can be used to help students communicate their ideas and thoughts in a clear and concise way. An example is that a teacher can prompt students to write a short message to a friend and ask ChatGPT to generate suggestions for making the message more effective. This could include comments such as "Use simpler vocabulary to make your message easier to understand." By providing students with suggestions for improving their communication, ChatGPT can help them become more effective communicators.

Promoting critical thinking

Using ChatGPT in the English language teaching (ELT) classroom can also promote critical thinking by challenging students to think about language and communication in new ways.

A teacher could prompt students to write a persuasive argument and ask ChatGPT to generate counterarguments. This not only helps students develop critical thinking skills, but also encourages them to consider multiple perspectives and become more effective communicators. The ability to think critically about language is an essential aspect of language learning and can help students to use language more effectively in a variety of contexts.

Supporting individualized learning

Another significant benefit of ChatGPT is its ability to support individualized learning. The model's prompt functionality can guide students towards writing or speaking about topics that align with their individual interests and abilities, keeping them motivated and engaged in the learning process. For instance, a teacher might prompt a student interested in science to write about a recent scientific advancement in English. ChatGPT can then provide customized feedback, such as "Great job explaining the concept! Try to include more examples to help the reader better understand." With its ability to adapt to each student's learning pace and language level, ChatGPT can support an effective and enjoyable language learning experience.

Encouraging collaboration and teamwork

ChatGPT can also be used to encourage collaboration and teamwork among students. By using the model's dialogue generation capabilities, teachers can facilitate group discussions and debates, helping students to develop their communication and critical thinking skills in a collaborative setting. An example of this is a debate between two groups of students and asking ChatGPT to play the role of the moderator, guiding the discussion and keeping the students on track. This not only promotes collaboration and teamwork, but also helps students build critical thinking skills by considering multiple perspectives.

ChatGPT offers a wealth of opportunities for English language teachers to enhance their teaching and engage students in new and creative ways. If you are looking for a tool to take your teaching to the next level, look no further than ChatGPT. By harnessing the power of cutting-edge technology, teachers can create dynamic, engaging, and personalized learning experiences for their students like never before. With ChatGPT as a tool, the possibilities for ELT classrooms are endless. It is time for teachers to embrace the future of education and take student learning.

Ask and You Shall Receive: Creating Effective Questions for ChatGPT

ChatGPT is a cutting-edge language model developed by OpenAI that has the capability to provide informative responses to a vast array of questions covering a wide spectrum of topics. Nonetheless, as with any AI-based chatbot, the quality of ChatGPT's answers is largely determined by the quality of the questions posed to it. It is, therefore, essential to know how to formulate effective and well-structured questions when interacting with ChatGPT.

Why effective questions?

To understand why making effective questions is important when using ChatGPT, you need to know how ChatGPT works. ChatGPT is a machine learning model that uses natural language processing (NLP) to understand and respond to questions. When you ask a question, ChatGPT analyzes the question's language and context to provide an appropriate response.

Hence, if the question is vague or ambiguous, ChatGPT may not be able to provide a relevant or accurate response. For example, if you ask "What's the meaning of life?", ChatGPT may give you a generic philosophical answer because the question is too broad and lacks specificity. On the other hand, if you ask "What is the scientific definition of life?", ChatGPT will give you a more specific and accurate response.

Characteristics of effective questions

As mentioned, ChatGPT has been designed to provide responses based on the questions that are asked. Therefore, it is important to consider certain characteristics when formulating questions to increase the likelihood of receiving effective and informative responses. To ensure that the responses received from ChatGPT are relevant and informative, questions should possess the following characteristics.

Clarity

The question should be clear and concise, without any ambiguity or vagueness. This helps ChatGPT understand the intent behind the question and provide a more accurate response.

"What is the main idea of this paragraph?"

This question is clear and straightforward, without any ambiguity or unnecessary information.

Specificity

The question should be specific and focused on a particular topic or subject. Broad or vague questions can be difficult for ChatGPT to provide effective responses to.

"What are the symptoms of COVID-19?"

This question is specific and focused on the particular topic COVID-19, making it easier for ChatGPT to provide relevant information.

Open-endedness

Open-ended questions that allow for multiple possible answers can help generate more thoughtful and creative responses from ChatGPT.

"What are some possible solutions to address deforestation?"

This open-ended question allows multiple possible answers and encourages ChatGPT to generate more thoughtful and creative responses.

Relevance

The question should be relevant to the expertise and capabilities of ChatGPT. As a language model, ChatGPT is designed to respond to questions about language and general knowledge, rather than specialized topics or fields such as medical diagnosis, legal advice, or financial planning. Personal or individualized advice and information are also not what ChatGPT is capable of responding effectively.

"What are the basic principles of algebra?""

This question is relevant to ChatGPT's expertise in providing general knowledge and information, rather than being too specialized or technical in nature.

Creating effective questions for ChatGPT

In order to help teachers get the most out of their interactions with ChatGPT, there are several tips that can be followed to ensure that the responses received are effective and informative. Following these guidelines can assist teachers in enhancing ChatGPT's ability to provide useful information and insights.

Be clear and specific: Avoid asking broad or vague questions. Instead, try to use precise and concise language to communicate your thoughts and intentions accurately.

Use correct terminology and language: To get accurate and relevant responses from ChatGPT, it is essential to use the correct terminology and language. This means using the appropriate vocabulary, grammar, and syntax when phrasing your questions.

Provide adequate context: When asking a question, it is essential to provide enough context to help ChatGPT understand the topic or subject you are asking about. This can include background information, relevant details, and any specific objectives or goals you have.

Vary your question types: Use a variety of question types to get the most out of ChatGPT. This can include open-ended, multiple choice, or true/false questions. These various types of questions can encourage ChatGPT to provide more thoughtful and creative responses.

Review responses critically: After receiving a response from ChatGPT, it is essential to review it critically to check its accuracy and relevance. If necessary, ask follow-up questions to clarify or expand upon the response. By doing so, you can ensure that you get the most out of ChatGPT and its capabilities.

ChatGPT is a highly versatile tool that can greatly facilitate both teaching and learning. To fully utilize its capabilities, it is crucial to formulate effective and precise questions that can yield accurate and relevant responses from ChatGPT. With well-structured queries, teachers and students can optimize their interactions with ChatGPT and extract the maximum benefits from this exceptional tool.

The Interpretation Game: Evaluating ChatGPT Responses

As AI technology continues to advance, AI language models like ChatGPT are gaining popularity across various industries, particularly in education. Thanks to its proficiency in generating text-based responses to a broad range of prompts, ChatGPT has proven to be a valuable tool for educators. It offers fast and efficient personalized responses that cater to specific needs. Nevertheless, as with any AI technology, it is critical to interpret and evaluate ChatGPT responses carefully to ensure their accuracy and relevance before putting them to use.

The significance of evaluating ChatGPT responses

ChatGPT is a powerful AI language model that can generate responses based on patterns in vast amounts of text data that it has been extensively trained on. When a user provides a prompt or question, ChatGPT carefully analyzes and interprets the input, grasps its context, and produces a response based on its understanding of the input and its acquired knowledge.

ChatGPT's ability to provide fast and personalized responses to student inquiries makes it an attractive technology for the education sector. However, there are certain risks associated with relying solely on ChatGPT responses. These risks include the possibility of ChatGPT providing inaccurate or biased responses, and overlooking the importance of human interaction in the educational process.

It is, therefore, recommended that teachers and students approach ChatGPT responses with a critical eye and use them in conjunction with human expertise. Proper interpretation and evaluation of ChatGPT responses can help to ensure their accuracy and relevance in the educational setting. The next section presents 10 strategies for teachers and students to use to interpret and evaluate ChatGPT responses.

Strategies for evaluating ChatGPT responses

Strategy	Explanation	Possible action
Considering the context of the question or prompt	ChatGPT responses are generated based on the language used in the prompt or question. Users should consider the context of the question or prompt to ensure that ChatGPT's response is relevant to the topic being discussed.	Asking ChatGPT "What is the capital of California?" instead of just "What is the capital?"
Identifying the underlying meaning or intent of the response	ChatGPT responses are created based on patterns found in its training data. It is important to identify the underlying meaning or intent behind the created text.	Identifying if a response is sarcastic or if it is promoting certain opinions or ideas.
Checking for factual accuracy and consistency	ChatGPT responses are not always accurate or consistent. Therefore, fact-checking responses for accuracy and consistency with credible sources before using them is vital.	Cross-referencing responses with trusted sources or consulting a subject-matter expert.
Analyzing the tone and style of the response	ChatGPT responses may have a particular tone or style that may be inappropriate or confusing in the educational setting. It is important to analyze the tone and style of the response and to adjust it accordingly.	Adjusting responses to be more professional or appropriate for the educational setting.

Strategy	Explanation	Possible action
Recognizing potential biases or limitations	ChatGPT responses may reflect biases or limitations found in its training data. Teachers and students should recognize these potential biases or limitations and address them.	Analyzing the tone and style of the response to identify biases or comparing responses to other sources to verify their accuracy.
Considering the target audience of the response	ChatGPT responses may be inappropriate or irrelevant for a particular target audience. It is always advisable to consider the target audience when interpreting ChatGPT responses.	Adjusting responses to be more age-appropriate or tailored to the intended audience.
Assessing the relevance and usefulness of the response	ChatGPT responses may be irrelevant or unhelpful in the educational setting. Always assess the relevance and usefulness of the response before using it.	Checking if the response directly answers the question or if it provides additional information.
Evaluating the quality of the language and grammar	ChatGPT responses may contain errors in grammar or language that may affect their readability or understanding. Do not forget to check the language and grammar before using the response.	Running the response through a grammar and spell-check program.
Testing the response for accuracy and completeness	ChatGPT responses may not always be accurate or complete. It is important to test the response for accuracy and completeness before using it.	Double-checking responses for any missing or doubtful information.

Strategy	Explanation	Possible action
Considering the potential consequences of using the response	ChatGPT responses may have consequences for students or educators if they are inaccurate or misleading. Remember to consider the potential consequences of using the response before incorporating it into educational materials or assessments.	Evaluating the potential impact of using the response and whether it could negatively affect students' learning outcomes.

ChatGPT has proven to be a magic tool for teachers and learners thanks to its ability to provide prompt and personalized answers to their questions. It is the users' job, however, to approach ChatGPT responses critically and to supplement them with human expertise. Properly interpreting and evaluating the information generated by ChatGPT can guarantee their accuracy and applicability in the educational context.

From Questions to Discoveries: Using ChatGPT to Drvie IBL Projects

As an AI language model trained by OpenAI, ChatGPT has the potential to support student learning and engagement through inquiry-based learning (IBL). IBL is an approach to learning that emphasizes student exploration, questioning, and investigation of a particular topic. With ChatGPT's ability to generate natural language responses, teachers and students can use it to make questions and explore a topic more deeply, making it an ideal tool for IBL projects. Let's see how teachers can help students to make the most of this learning approach.

Setting up ChatGPT for IBL

To set up ChatGPT for use in teaching, you will need to provide students with access to the platform and ensure they are familiar with how to use it effectively. There are a few tips you can follow to optimize this process.

Explain the purpose of using ChatGPT: It is important to explain to students why you are incorporating ChatGPT into the classroom. Let them know how the technology can be used to facilitate learning and inquiry, and how it can help them generate new questions and ideas.

Provide students with access to ChatGPT: ChatGPT is available and you need to sign up for an account to use it. Once you have an account, you can provide students with access to the platform.

Familiarize students with ChatGPT: Before incorporating ChatGPT into IBL projects, you will want to ensure that students are familiar with how to use the platform. Providing a brief introduction to the platform and some basic guidelines for generating questions with ChatGPT is necessary.

Discuss ethical concerns: As with any technology, there are ethical concerns surrounding the use of ChatGPT. For example, students may need to be reminded that ChatGPT is an AI language model, not a human, and that it may not always provide accurate or unbiased information. It is highly recommended that you discuss these concerns with students and provide guidelines for using ChatGPT ethically and responsibly.

Provide guidelines for making effective questions and prompts: As students use ChatGPT to generate questions and ideas, they need to know how to do so effectively. You may want to encourage students to use open-ended questions, to consider multiple perspectives, and to evaluate the quality of the information they receive.

Using ChatGPT for Inquiry-Based Learning

Once you have set up ChatGPT for use in teaching, you can begin incorporating it into IBL projects. Here are some tips for using ChatGPT in class for IBL.

Select a topic that can benefit from using ChatGPT: You have to identify a subject or issue that can be explored through inquiry and questioning, not one that is too simple. ChatGPT can help students generate new and varied questions that can lead to deeper understanding of the topic. Let's say that you want to explore the topic of climate change with your students. This is a complex and multifaceted topic that can help students ask more in-depth questions.

Use ChatGPT to generate questions and explore the topic: To get started, you could prompt students to enter a question related to climate change into ChatGPT. For example, a student might enter the question, "What are the primary causes of climate change?" ChatGPT would generate a response, which might include information about greenhouse gas emissions, deforestation, and other factors. Students can then use this information as a starting point for further research and exploration.

Encourage students to use ChatGPT as a tool for further research and investigation: As students generate questions and explore the topic, they can continue to use ChatGPT as a tool for further research and investigation. For example, a student might enter the question,

"How do greenhouse gas emissions impact the environment?" ChatGPT could generate a response, which might include information about the effects of greenhouse gases on the atmosphere, oceans, and ecosystems. Students can use this information to develop a deeper understanding of the topic and identify additional areas for research.

Provide guidance on how to use ChatGPT effectively: This is a critical step that helps ensure students are getting the most out of the platform when exploring the topic. You might provide guidelines for avoiding biased or incomplete sources and tips for evaluating the information generated by ChatGPT in the context of climate change. You could also encourage students to use other sources in addition to ChatGPT to ensure that they are getting a well-rounded understanding of the topic.

Monitor student progress and offer feedback to support learning: This step is also critical as students always need you to monitor their progress and offer feedback to support their work. For example, you might review their questions and research related to climate change and provide feedback on areas for improvement or additional areas to explore. You could also offer suggestions for additional resources or materials related to climate change that might help them deepen their understanding of the topic.

Help students use ChatGPT to create a presentation: After students have explored the topic of climate change using ChatGPT, they can use the information they have gathered to create a presentation. ChatGPT might help them create a PowerPoint presentation that summarizes their findings and includes visuals to help communicate their ideas. As a teacher, you can guide through the process of creating an effective presentation and encourage students to use ChatGPT to generate additional information and insights to include in their presentation.

Assist students in using ChatGPT to self-reflect on their project: Students can use ChatGPT to self-reflect on their work after they finish their project. For example, they might enter a question such as "How effective was my presentation on climate change?" and receive ChatGPT's feedback and suggestions for improvement. Again, at this step, you can guide through the process. This step can help students develop their self-assessment skills and complete the IBL process in a successful way.

> **Incorporating ChatGPT into IBL projects can bring a dynamic and engaging element to the classroom. By supporting students in exploring, questioning, and investigating specific topics, ChatGPT can empower students to take ownership of their own learning journey, enhancing their learning outcomes and encouraging them to become active and curious learners, who are equipped to succeed in an increasingly complex and interconnected world.**

ChatGPT: A Teacher's Secret Weapon for Lesson Planning

Planning lessons for teaching can be a daunting and time-consuming task that requires a lot of effort and attention to detail. Teachers often face challenges such as a lack of time, resources, and creativity. However, with the help of AI technology, teachers can now use natural language processing tools to compose lesson plans with greater ease and efficiency, regardless of the challenges they may face. One such tool is ChatGPT, a language model trained by OpenAI that can generate natural language text based on a given prompt. Thanks to ChatGPT, teachers can create detailed and high-quality lesson plans in a more streamlined manner, without having to spend excessive amounts of time and energy on planning, while also ensuring that their plans are tailored to the needs of their students.

To get started with ChatGPT, you will need to sign up for an account and log in. Once you are logged in, you will be able to access the interface and select the appropriate model and prompt for your lesson plan.

Composing lesson plans with ChatGPT

Now that you are familiar with ChatGPT, let's get started with composing a lesson plan. Suppose we want to teach our students the present perfect tense in English. Here's how we can use ChatGPT to compose a lesson plan.

- **Step 1:** Open the ChatGPT interface.

- **Step 2:** Enter the prompt. For example, *"Compose a 5E lesson plan for teaching the present perfect tense to intermediate-level ELT students."*

  Giving a concise and detailed prompt for ChatGPT is crucial if you want it to suggest a usable lesson plan. You need to let

ChatGPT know exactly what you are looking for, and the more information you provide, the more accurate and effective its suggestions will be. In this case, we have specified that we are looking for a 5E lesson plan that covers the present perfect tense and is suitable for intermediate-level English language teaching (ELT) students. This level of detail allows ChatGPT to generate a lesson plan that is tailored to the specific needs and abilities of the target audience.

- **Step 3:** ChatGPT will generate a response based on the prompt, providing ideas for the lesson plan, examples, and activities. Here's an example response generated by ChatGPT (note that the table format of the lesson plan can also be automatically generated by ChatGPT if you ask it to do it in your prompt). Let's look at the lesson plan generated by ChatGPT.

Lesson Plan for teaching the Present Perfect Tense

Objective: By the end of this lesson, students will be able to use the present perfect tense correctly in sentences and in familiar contexts.

(Continued on the next page.)

Phase	Activity	Objective	Materials	Assessment
Engage	**Brainstorming** Teachers provide a list of experiences such as traveling to Paris, eating Vietnamese Phở, going camping, etc. and ask students to talk to friends which one they did in the past. After a few minutes of discussion, bring the class back together and ask a few students to share their partner/group's experiences with the class. Use their responses to model sentences in the present perfect tense. Give students an opportunity to ask questions about the present perfect tense and practice using it themselves.	To activate prior knowledge and generate interest in the topic	Whiteboard and markers	Observation and discussion
Explore	**Scavenger Hunt** Students will work in pairs or small groups to complete a scavenger hunt activity, using laptops or mobile devices to search for examples of the present perfect tense in real-life contexts (e.g. news articles, social media posts, etc.). They will then record their findings on a worksheet, identifying the form and function of each example.	To explore real-life uses of the present perfect tense	Worksheets, laptops or mobile devices with internet access	Completion of the worksheet

Phase	Activity	Objective	Materials	Assessment
Explain	**Grammar Lesson** The teacher will lead a mini-lesson on the form and function of the present perfect tense, using examples from the scavenger hunt activity to illustrate key points. Students will receive a handout that summarizes the main rules and structures of the present perfect tense, and they will complete a brief exercise to reinforce their understanding.	To explain the form and function of the present perfect tense	Whiteboard, markers, handouts	Completion of the handout
Elaborate	**Story Short Writing** Students will use writing prompts provided by the teacher to create their own short stories that incorporate the present perfect tense. They will focus on using the tense correctly and meaningfully, and will strive to create vivid and engaging narratives. Once completed, students will share their stories with the class.	To practice using the present perfect tense in a creative context	Writing prompts, paper, pencils	Completed stories

Phase	Activity	Objective	Materials	Assessment
Evaluate	**Peer review** Students will exchange their stories with a partner, who will read and evaluate the story using a rubric provided by the teacher. They will then provide constructive feedback to their partner, focusing on areas where the present perfect tense was used correctly and areas where it could be improved.	To assess students' understanding and correct any mistakes	Completed stories, rubric	Peer evaluations and feedback

ChatGPT has the ability to tailor a lesson plan to your specific preferences in terms of lesson format, duration, types of activities, steps and stages, etc. However, you need to provide clear instructions in your prompt so that ChatGPT can accurately meet your expectations.

- **Step 4:** Use the response generated by ChatGPT as a starting point and modify the lesson plan to suit your students' needs. For example, you might want to add additional examples or activities to reinforce the concept of the present perfect tense, or if most of your students are visual learners, you can ask ChatGPT to modify the activities to match them for you.

Fine-tuning lesson plans with ChatGPT

After ChatGPT has created the lesson plan, let's fine-tune it to suit the needs of our students. Suppose we have a class of advanced-level ELT students who are already familiar with the present perfect tense. Below is what ChatGPT may suggest.

"To modify the lesson plan for advanced-level ELT students, consider the following:

Increase the complexity of the examples: Instead of simple sentences, use more complex sentences that require a deeper understanding of the present perfect tense. For example, "I have never been to Paris, but I have visited other cities in France."

Increase the level of abstraction: Challenge students to apply the present perfect tense to more abstract or complex concepts, such as discussing trends or changes in society, economics, or technology. This will require more nuanced understanding and application of the tense.

Incorporate more advanced grammar concepts: For example, you could introduce the past participle or the difference between the present perfect and past simple tenses."

Then you can use the suggestions generated by ChatGPT to modify the lesson plan accordingly. For example, you could modify the activities to have students create longer, more complex stories or dialogues that incorporate the present perfect tense.

You can even ask ChatGPT to modify the whole lesson plan for you. Here's an example of a modified lesson plan to teach the present perfect tense for advanced-level students suggested by ChatGPT.

Phase	Activity	Objective	Materials	Assessment
Engage	**Discussion** Students will engage in a group discussion on the present perfect tense, drawing on their prior knowledge to identify patterns and common usage. The teacher will guide the discussion and encourage students to explore more complex aspects of the tense.	To activate prior knowledge and generate interest in the topic	Whiteboard and markers	Observation and discussion
Explore	**Real-life Applications** Students will analyze authentic examples of the present perfect tense in use, drawn from sources such as news articles, academic papers, or literary works. They will discuss the nuances of the tense and identify patterns in usage, considering factors such as register, context, and authorial intent.	To explore authentic uses of the present perfect tense	Texts, laptops or mobile devices with internet access	Discussion and analysis

Phase	Activity	Objective	Materials	Assessment
Explain	**Grammar Review** The teacher will lead a review of the key rules and structures of the present perfect tense, with a focus on more complex aspects of the tense such as the present perfect for past actions with present relevance. Students will receive a handout that summarizes the main points of the review, and they will complete a brief exercise to reinforce their understanding.	To review the key rules and structures of the present perfect tense	Whiteboard, markers, handouts	Completion of the handout
Elaborate	**Debate** Students will participate in a structured debate on a topic such as the merits of wearing uniforms to school. They will use the tense effectively and persuasively, and will strive to incorporate more advanced structures and patterns in their arguments. The teacher will act as a moderator and provide feedback on students' use of the tense.	To practice using the present perfect tense in a more complex and structured context	Debate prompts, timer	Performance in the debate

Phase	Activity	Objective	Materials	Assessment
Evaluate	**Writing Assignment** Students will complete a writing assignment that requires them to use the present perfect tense in a more sophisticated and nuanced way, such as describing a complex series of events or reflecting on a personal experience. They will focus on using the tense effectively and meaningfully, and will strive to incorporate more advanced structures and patterns in their writing. The teacher will assess the completed assignments and provide feedback to the students.	To assess students' understanding and ability to use the present perfect tense in a more sophisticated context	Writing prompts, paper, pencils	Completed writing assignments

Creating lesson plans with ChatGPT based on a textbook lesson

ChatGPT can not only assist teachers in creating a lesson plan from scratch but also aid in developing a lesson plan based on a textbook lesson. Below are some useful tips to consider.

Identify key themes and topics: Review your lesson from the textbook and identify the key themes and topics that it covers. Consider which of these topics you want to focus on in your lesson plans, and what specific learning objectives you want to achieve with each lesson.

Generate ideas for activities and assessments: Once you have identified the key topics and learning objectives for your lessons, use ChatGPT to generate ideas for activities and assessments that align with these objectives. You can input prompts such as "What are some engaging activities that would help students practice using the present perfect tense?" or "What are some effective ways to assess student understanding of complex sentence structures?" for ideas.

Adapt the generated content to your textbook: Review the generated ideas and adapt them to your textbook as needed. Make sure that the activities and assessments you have selected align with the content and objectives of your textbook, and that they provide appropriate scaffolding and support for your students.

Sequence the activities: Once you have developed a set of activities and assessments for each lesson, sequence them in a logical and coherent way. Consider how each activity builds on the previous one, and how the activities and assessments are scaffolded to support student learning.

Refine and revise: As you implement your lesson plans, be prepared to refine and revise them based on student feedback and your own observations of student learning. Use ChatGPT to generate new ideas and activities as needed, and make adjustments to the sequencing and pacing of the lessons as necessary.

Below are some practical ideas for teachers to use ChatGPT with textbook contents. Applying these ideas can help you to create a rich and varied learning experience for your students.

Generating exercises: ChatGPT can be used to generate exercises that align with the content of your textbook. You can input prompts such as "Create a fill-in-the-blank exercise that focuses on the present perfect tense," or you can input a reading passage from the textbook and ask ChatGPT to "generate 5 comprehension questions for this reading text".

Generating discussion or writing prompts: ChatGPT can generate discussion or writing prompts for your class activities. For instance, you can input prompts such as "Generate discussion/ writing prompts that help students reflect on their understanding of the present perfect tense." ChatGPT can then generate a variety of prompts that you can use to encourage students to engage deeply with the content of your textbook.

Providing assessment support: ChatGPT can help you create assessments that align with the content of your textbook. Just input prompts such as "Create a short-answer assessment that requires students to demonstrate their understanding of the present perfect tense," and ChatGPT can then generate assessments that you can use to evaluate student understanding and progress.

Suggesting games or activities: ChatGPT can also be used to suggest games or activities for your textbook lessons. With prompts like "What are some games or activities that will help students practice irregular verbs?", or "Suggest an activity that will help students understand the difference between simple past and present perfect tense," you will receive a variety of games or activities that you can use to make learning more engaging and enjoyable for your students.

Creating worksheets: You can easily create worksheets that align with the content of your textbook with the help of ChatGPT. For example, you can input prompts such as "Create a vocabulary worksheet about the topic Occupations for Fifth graders," or "Generate a worksheet for students to review the contents of Module 3." (Certainly you have to let ChatGPT know the contents of Module 3 in advance.) ChatGPT can then generate ready-made worksheets that you can use in class.

[Module 3 Revision]
Student Name: _________________
Class Info: _________________

Exercise 1: Fill in the Blank
Complete the following sentences with the appropriate form of the verb in parentheses.
   1. I _____ (play) soccer every Saturday with my friends.
   2. She _____ (study) English for three years.
   3. They _____ (not eat) meat because they are vegetarians.
   4. We _____ (travel) to Europe last summer.
   5. He _____ (not finish) his homework yet.

Exercise 2: Matching
Match the following vocabulary words with their definitions.
   1. culture
   2. archaeologist
   3. tradition
   4. heritage
   5. community

   a. a person who studies the past
   b. a group of people who share a language and culture
   c. a set of beliefs, customs, and practices
   d. the study of ancient societies and artifacts
   e. something that is passed down from previous generations

Exercise 3: Short Answer
Answer the following questions in complete sentences.
   1. What is your favorite type of food? Why?
   2. Have you ever traveled outside of your country? Where did you go and what did you do there?
   3. What are your favorite hobbies? Why do you enjoy them?

Exercise 4: Writing
Write a short paragraph describing your favorite place in your city or town. Include details about the location, the atmosphere, and why you enjoy spending time there.

____
____
____
____
____
____
____

** This worksheet was entirely generated by ChatGPT.*

Utilizing ChatGPT for lesson planning, teachers can creatively transform the way they prepare their teaching material. With ChatGPT's advanced language processing abilities, teachers can quickly and effortlessly generate customized lesson plans that cater to the specific learning preferences and needs of their students. Not only does this save valuable time and energy, but it also results in more engaging and stimulating lessons that are bound to captivate and inspire students. It can be seen that ChatGPT has empowered teachers to elevate the quality of their teaching and maximize their students' learning potential.

Human Touch: ChatGPT as a Tool, Not a Replacement

Technology has transformed education by offering new tools and resources to enhance teaching and learning. Among these tools is OpenAI's ChatGPT, a powerful language model recommended for teachers and students in almost all learning environments. However, it is crucial to remember that technology should never replace the importance of human interaction and connection in education. As teachers integrate ChatGPT into their teaching practices, they must find ways to balance the benefits of technology with the essential human touch that is essential for student engagement, motivation, and success. Remember that ChatGPT is a tool, not a replacement, for human touch.

Why human touch matters

In today's fast-paced, technology-driven world, it can be easy to overlook the significance of human touch in education. However, human touch remains a critical component of effective teaching and learning, and is essential for building strong relationships between teachers and students.

Human touch can take many forms, including physical touch, verbal communication, and emotional support. Physical touch, such as a handshake, high-five, or pat on the back, can help to establish a sense of connection and trust between teachers and students, and promote a positive classroom culture. Verbal communication, such as offering praise, encouragement, or constructive feedback, can reinforce positive behavior and motivate students to strive for excellence. Emotional support, such as listening, empathizing, and providing a safe and supportive learning environment, can promote student well-being and mental health.

Research has shown that human touch can have a profound impact on student learning and development. Positive teacher-student relationships can lead to improved academic performance, increased motivation, and higher levels of engagement in the classroom (Hamre & Pianta, 2005; McCormick et al., 2013; Pekrun, R. et al., 2017). Additionally, strong teacher-student relationships have been linked to improved student behavior and reduced rates of discipline problems (O'Connor & McCartney, 2007).

Human touch is particularly important for vulnerable or marginalized students, such as those from low-income backgrounds, students with disabilities, or students who have experienced trauma. These students may face additional barriers to academic success, and may benefit from the emotional support and encouragement that human touch can provide.

In short, it is clear that human touch matters in education because it is essential for building strong teacher-student relationships, promoting positive classroom culture, and supporting student learning and development. In today's era of technology, though Edtech tools like ChatGPT can be a valuable addition for education, they should not be relied on as a replacement for human touch.

Strategies for infusing a human touch into ChatGPT

ChatGPT can be utilized as a teaching tool for educators looking to improve their teaching and create a more personalized, engaging, and inclusive learning experience for their students, while still maintaining a human touch. The power of AI will help teachers enhance their ability to create meaningful interactions and build strong teacher-student relationships. Below are some strategies for teachers to effectively infuse a human touch into utilizing ChatGPT in their lessons.

Provide personalized feedback: Teachers can use ChatGPT to provide personalized feedback to students on their assignments or projects. With ChatGPT, feedback is tailored for each student and focuses on areas where they may be struggling or where they have shown improvement. This helps students feel seen and heard, and cared for on a personal level.

Provide real-time feedback: ChatGPT can also provide real-time feedback to students during classes. Teachers can use ChatGPT to respond to student questions or comments, and to provide additional information or clarification. This is specifically helpful to create a sense of immediacy and engagement in the online classroom, where teacher-student interactions and relationships may be limited.

Encourage collaboration: Teachers can utilize ChatGPT for facilitating collaboration and group work among students. Teachers can encourage students to work together on ChatGPT-based assignments and activities. Students can even use and treat ChatGPT as one of their group members and collaborate with it to complete the assignment.

Offer emotional support: ChatGPT can be used as a tool for teachers to offer emotional support to students who may be struggling with personal or academic issues. Teachers can use ChatGPT to check in on students and offer words of encouragement or support. This is particularly beneficial for students who may be experiencing feelings of isolation or disconnection from their peers.

Recommend additional and personalized resources: Teachers can make use of ChatGPT to provide additional resources to students on specific topics or assignments or based on student learning needs and styles. This helps students to feel supported in their learning, which can lead to increased student learning engagement and motivation.

Foster communication: Communication is key to building strong relationships with students and maintaining a human touch in the classroom. Teachers can use ChatGPT to promote communication with their students and between students, fostering a sense of community and connection in the classroom.

Provide opportunities for reflection and self-assessment: Teachers can ask students to use ChatGPT to reflect on their learning, identify areas where they need support or improvement, and set goals for themselves. By doing this, students take an active role in their own learning, which can strengthen a sense of ownership and engagement that goes beyond traditional classroom settings.

Integrate social and emotional learning: Teachers can integrate social and emotional learning (SEL) into their curriculum by using ChatGPT to facilitate SEL activities and discussions. This creates chances for students to develop important social and emotional skills, such as empathy, communication, and problem-solving, which can improve their overall well-being and academic success.

Balancing ChatGPT use with other learning strategies

It is clear that ChatGPT can effectively support learning and teaching, but it is also important to use it in balance with other learning strategies to ensure a well-rounded education for students. Here are some reasons why incorporating multiple learning approaches is crucial.

First, ChatGPT is a machine, and does not provide the same level of human interaction and emotion as a teacher or peer. Balancing ChatGPT use with other learning strategies makes teachers promote a human touch in students' learning, help students build relationships with teachers and peers, and foster a sense of community and belonging in the classroom.

Second, students have different learning styles, and relying solely on ChatGPT can limit their opportunities to engage with other learning strategies that cater to different learning styles. Teachers need to incorporate different learning approaches and activities, such as visual aids, group activities, and hands-on learning to guarantee that students have access to a variety of learning styles and strategies that support their individual needs.

Third, while ChatGPT can provide students with precious support in academic areas, it may not necessarily teach them the real-world skills they need to succeed in their future careers. Other learning strategies, such as project-based learning or gamification, will help students develop real-world skills that will benefit them beyond the classroom.

Last, but very important, utilizing a variety of teaching strategies will help teachers address equity and inclusivity in their teaching. In reality, ChatGPT may not be available to all students due to technological or financial barriers. Teachers incorporating other learning strategies gives all students access to learning opportunities and promotes a sense of belonging for students regardless of their background or access to technology.

Despite the fact that ChatGPT can be beneficial to teaching and learning, it is not a magic wand to solve all educational challenges. It is important for teachers to use ChatGPT in conjunction with other teaching strategies and approaches to provide a well-rounded education for their students, including ensuring the human factors of education. Infusing a human touch into their teaching practices assists teachers to build strong relationships with their students, promote a positive classroom culture, and support student learning and development. Just remember, ChatGPT is a machine, not a replacement for humans.

References

Hamre, B. K., & Pianta, R. C. (2005). Can instructional and emotional support in the first-grade classroom make a difference for children at risk of school failure?. *Child Development, 76(5), 949-967.*

O'Connor, E., & McCartney, K. (2007). Examining teacher-child relationships and achievement as part of an ecological model of development. *American Educational Research Journal, 44, 340-369.*

McCormick, M. P. et al. (2013). Teacher–child relationships and academic achievement: A multilevel propensity score model approach. *Journal of School Psychology, 51, 611–624.*

Pekrun, R. et al. (2017). Achievement Emotions and Academic Performance: Longitudinal Models of Reciprocal Effects. *Child Dev., 88(5),1653-1670.*

Incorporating ChatGPT in Your Lessons: Tips and Strategies

As technology continues to advance, educators are finding new ways to enhance the learning experience of their students. One tool that has shown great potential in the classroom is ChatGPT, a language model developed by OpenAI. With its ability to generate text in a wide range of subjects and styles, ChatGPT can be a valuable resource for teachers looking to incorporate technology into their lessons. However, in order to use it effectively, what are the recommendations for teachers and what are some words of caution regarding what to steer clear of?

Recommendations for teachers on utilizing ChatGPT

Recommendation	Explanation	Example
Use ChatGPT as a research tool	Teachers can use ChatGPT to find answers to questions, gather information on a topic, or explore different areas of interest.	A teacher can ask ChatGPT to provide details about the key events and figures of the Roman Empire.
Use ChatGPT for brainstorming	Teachers can ask ChatGPT to generate ideas, titles, or thesis statements that can spark creativity and inspire students.	A teacher can ask ChatGPT to generate a list of possible angles for a writing task on the topic of climate change, such as the impact on wildlife, the role of technology, or the political implications.

Recommendation	Explanation	Example
Use ChatGPT for writing prompts	Teachers can ask ChatGPT to generate prompts for creative writing, essays, or research papers.	A teacher can ask ChatGPT to generate a list of possible questions for a research paper on the topic of artificial intelligence, such as "What are the ethical implications of AI in healthcare?" or "How has AI impacted the job market?"
Use ChatGPT for language learning	Teachers can ask ChatGPT to generate sentences, paragraphs, or dialogues in different languages, which can help students practice their language skills.	A teacher can ask ChatGPT to generate a conversation between two people ordering food at a restaurant in French, using the target idioms for a lesson on French idioms.
Use ChatGPT for quiz and game creation	Teachers can ask ChatGPT to design interactive quizzes and games that assess students' comprehension and familiarity with a subject.	A teacher can ask ChatGPT to create a quiz containing queries like "What is the symbol for carbon?" or "Which element belongs to the noble gas group?" to test their pupils on the periodic table's elements.
Use ChatGPT for virtual conversations	Teachers can ask ChatGPT to generate dialogues, debates, or role-playing scenarios that require students to use language in context.	A teacher can ask ChatGPT to generate a scenario where two people are trying to agree on a price for a used car to help their students practice negotiating skills.

Recommendation	Explanation	Example
Use ChatGPT for personalized learning	Teachers can ask ChatGPT to generate content, resources, or activities that are tailored to students' needs and interests.	A teacher can ask ChatGPT to generate a series of grammar exercises that target the specific weaknesses of a student struggling with grammar.
Use ChatGPT for feedback and evaluation	Teachers can ask ChatGPT to generate feedback based on specific criteria or rubrics, which can save time and provide consistent and objective feedback.	A teacher can ask ChatGPT to generate feedback on the organization, clarity, and coherence of an essay submitted by a student and suggest corresponding interventions.

Cautionary considerations for teachers

While ChatGPT can be a valuable asset in the classroom, teachers must exercise caution when integrating it into their lessons. They should not rely solely on ChatGPT as a source of information or instruction, and should avoid over-reliance on the tool. Instead, teachers should combine it with other materials, such as textbooks, articles, and classroom discussions, to provide a comprehensive learning experience.

Teachers should also be aware of potential language limitations and inaccuracies in the responses provided by ChatGPT. As such, they should use their own judgment to evaluate and verify the accuracy of the information provided. Additionally, teachers should monitor student engagement with ChatGPT and adjust their use of the tool as necessary to ensure that it is contributing to positive learning outcomes.

It is crucial for teachers to exercise critical thinking and ethical considerations when utilizing ChatGPT, and ensure that student privacy is protected. Misusing or abusing ChatGPT in the classroom should be avoided, and teachers should discourage students from using it for plagiarism, as this can impede their academic progress and undermine the integrity of the learning process. Furthermore, teachers should be aware of the potential for bias and inappropriate content when using ChatGPT and take necessary steps to minimize these risks.

ChatGPT presents an exceptional opportunity for teachers to revolutionize their teaching practices by integrating technology into their lesson plans, which helps elevate the educational experience of their students and enables them to excel academically. Nonetheless, while ChatGPT is a valuable resource, it should be used in combination with other tools and materials to establish a comprehensive and dynamic approach to teaching and learning, providing an unparalleled educational experience to students.

Top Seven Mistakes to Avoid When Using ChatGPT in Education

ChatGPT is an AI language model with an array of exceptional applications, spanning from content creation to language translation. As with any powerful tool, its optimal use is dependent on the user's awareness of potential missteps. Therefore, it is important to refrain from these 7 common mistakes when utilizing ChatGPT. To ensure the most efficient and effective utilization of its capabilities.

#1 mistake: Treating ChatGPT as a human

One of the biggest mistakes that users make when using ChatGPT is treating it as if it were a human being. While ChatGPT is an advanced AI language model, it is not capable of understanding human language in the same way that humans do. It may not be able to pick up on the nuances of language or understand the context in the same way that a human would. Users should not expect ChatGPT to have emotions or personal opinions, and should not engage with it as if it were a person. Therefore, teachers and students should avoid expecting ChatGPT to function like a human, and instead recognize its limitations as an AI tool.

#2 mistake: Not providing enough context

One of the common errors that people make while using ChatGPT is failing to provide adequate context, which in turn can cause the tool to generate inaccurate responses. ChatGPT is an advanced language model that can produce responses that are customized to the specific query or question being asked. However, to achieve optimal results, ChatGPT relies heavily on contextual information. Without sufficient context, it can be challenging for ChatGPT to correctly interpret the intent behind a question or conversation, which may result in responses that are irrelevant or entirely unrelated. Consequently, it is vital for both teachers and students to provide appropriate context when using ChatGPT. This might include offering relevant background information, defining key terms or concepts, or providing examples that clarify the nature of the conversation.

#3 mistake: Not reviewing responses

Although ChatGPT is an innovative language model, it is subject to limitations and may generate incorrect or inappropriate responses due to the possible limited training data. Consequently, it is vital for users to approach ChatGPT with a critical eye and evaluate the responses generated carefully. Teachers, in particular, should be aware of the limitations of the system and use their professional judgment and expertise to verify that the responses are accurate and appropriate for their specific teaching contexts.

#4 mistake: Over relying on ChatGPT

ChatGPT is undoubtedly a valuable resource for learning and problem-solving. However, it is important to note that it should not be treated as a panacea for all academic and intellectual pursuits. In particular, when it comes to complex or sensitive topics, teachers should encourage their students to exercise their own critical thinking and decision-making abilities. ChatGPT can certainly provide useful information and perspectives, but it should not be relied upon exclusively, as it is still limited by the data and algorithms that inform its functioning. Instead, students should learn to question and evaluate the information provided by ChatGPT, and to supplement it with their own knowledge and insights.

#5 mistake: Not using proper grammar and spelling

As a language model, ChatGPT relies on the input it receives to generate responses. Hence, teachers must emphasize the significance of proper grammar and spelling when interacting with ChatGPT. Proper grammar and spelling ensure that ChatGPT responses are accurate, coherent, and easily understandable. On the other hand, using incorrect grammar and spelling can lead to confusion or irrelevant responses, which can be frustrating for both the teacher and the student. The use of slang or colloquialisms should also be avoided as ChatGPT may not understand their meaning, which may lead to inaccurate responses. For those reasons, teachers should encourage students to use complete sentences when interacting with ChatGPT.

This will help the language model better understand the context of the conversation and generate more relevant and accurate responses.

#6 mistake: Not being clear and concise

When engaging with a language model like ChatGPT, it is essential for users to communicate their questions and concerns in a clear and concise manner. The quality of the responses generated by ChatGPT heavily relies on the quality of the inputs. Vague or over-complicated input may result in irrelevant or inaccurate responses, leading to frustration and confusion for the users. To avoid such a situation, teachers and students should take care to formulate their questions and statements in a clear and straightforward way. This means avoiding excessively long sentences or using overly complex language that may be difficult for ChatGPT to comprehend.

#7 mistake: Not understanding how ChatGPT works

It is highly recommended that both educators and learners take the initiative to gain an in-depth understanding of ChatGPT and its functionality. Such knowledge would enable them to fully comprehend the extent of its capabilities, as well as its limitations, and how it generates responses. Doing this, students can take advantage of the tool's vast capabilities and optimize their interactions with it, allowing for a more fruitful and fulfilling learning experience. This would also aid in avoiding any potential misunderstandings or errors that may arise during usage.

ChatGPT provides cutting-edge solutions for teachers and students across a variety of tasks. However, it is crucial to bear in mind that ChatGPT does have its limitations. To avoid common pitfalls, users should exercise care and caution. Understanding these limitations and implementing appropriate measures will help to optimize the benefits of ChatGPT in teaching and learning. As such, it is imperative to utilize this tool with prudence and mindfulness to ensure seamless integration into educational environments.

Afterword

As we come to the end of this book, it is evident that the integration of ChatGPT in education can mark a new era in the field. ChatGPT has been shown to offer numerous benefits, including personalized learning, reducing teacher workload, and enhancing student engagement and motivation. Nevertheless, like any technology, ChatGPT has limitations and ethical considerations that need to be addressed.

In this book, we have examined ChatGPT in depth, from its evolution in education to its potential uses in teaching and learning. We have discovered how it can empower learners, help teachers plan lessons, and modernize school operations. And also, we have explored numerous practical ideas, tips, and strategies for educators and students to use ChatGPT effectively, as well as debunked myths surrounding its use and identified common mistakes to avoid.

While ChatGPT offers many advantages, it should not replace the human touch in education. As educators, we must embrace ChatGPT as a tool to support teaching and learning, but also remember that it is not a substitute for genuine human interaction and empathy. We must remain mindful of the ethical considerations associated with its use, such as data privacy, fairness, and accountability.

As we move forward in this brave new world of education, we must continue to explore the potential of ChatGPT and other emerging technologies. However, we should also remain critical and reflective, evaluating their impact on teaching and learning, and ensuring that they serve the best interests of our students and society.

In conclusion, the author hopes that this book has provided a comprehensive overview of ChatGPT in education, and has given you the ideas, tools, and knowledge to incorporate it into your teaching and learning practices efficiently. Thank you, and hope you have enjoyed reading this book. Wishing you all the best as you navigate this exciting new era in education to bring the best to our students.

Le Dinh Bao Quoc *(Author)*

About the Author

Le Dinh Bao Quoc

Le Dinh Bao Quoc is an experienced English Language Teaching professional with a Doctorate in Education. He founded Pro.Ed Education Solutions, which provides educational solutions for schools and institutes. Dr. Quoc is interested in using EdTech to improve teaching and learning outcomes, and his research areas include educational management, teacher professional development, and the impact of EdTech on education. He strongly believes in the power of education to change the world and is passionate about making a positive impact through education.

9 789358 462401